D0712902

DREAM WEAVER

JEREMY P. TARCHER/PENGUIN

a member of Penguin Group (USA)

New York

DREAM WEAVER

a memoir

MUSIC, MEDITATION, AND

MY FRIENDSHIP WITH

GEORGE HARRISON

GARY WRIGHT

JEREMY P. TARCHER/PENGUIN
Published by the Penguin Group
Penguin Group (USA) LLC
375 Hudson Street
New York, New York 10014

USA · Canada · UK · Ireland · Australia
New Zealand · India · South Africa · China

penguin.com
A Penguin Random House Company

Most Tarcher/Penguin books are available at special quantity discounts for bulk purchase for
sales promotions, premiums, fund-raising, and educational needs. Special books or book excerpts
also can be created to fit specific needs. For details, write: Special.Markets@us.penguingroup.com.

Library of Congress Cataloging-in-Publication Data

Wright, Gary.
Dream weaver : a memoir; music, meditation, and
my friendship with George Harrison / Gary Wright.
p. cm.
ISBN 978-0-399-16523-8 (hardback)
1. Wright, Gary, 1945– 2. Rock musicians—United States—Biography.
3. Harrison, George, 1943–2001—Friends and associates. I. Title.
ML420.W754 2014 2014026460
782.42166092—dc23

Printed in the United States of America
1 3 5 7 9 10 8 6 4 2

Book design by Meighan Cavanaugh

CONTENTS

Dream Weaver

I've just closed my eyes again
Climbed aboard the dream weaver train
Driver take away my worries of today
And leave tomorrow behind

Ooooh, dream weaver
I believe you can get me through the night
Ooooh, dream weaver
I believe we can reach the morning light

Fly me high through the starry skies
Or maybe to an astral plane
Cross the highways of fantasy
Help me to forget today's pain

Ooooh, dream weaver
I believe you can get me through the night
Ooooh, dream weaver
I believe we can reach the morning light

Though the dawn may be coming soon
There still may be some time
Fly me away to the bright side of the moon
And meet me on the other side

Ooooh, dream weaver
I believe you can get me through the night
Ooooh, dream weaver
I believe we can reach the morning light

PROLOGUE

God can be said to be the Weaver of Dreams in His vast creation, entertaining both Himself and mankind as He weaves epic stories and colossal events that span across lifetimes and millennia. In India, they say that running creation is God's eternal work and that He takes it very seriously—being a God of love and compassion rather than a punishing dictator. He gave man free will to create his own destiny, never interfering in an individual's life unless petitioned by pure love from His devotee.

On a human level, it can be said that each one of us is also a dream weaver, creating our own dreams and weaving our own lives over many incarnations, like actors in a movie playing roles as superstars or failures, heroes or villains—all of which are an integral part of His megadrama of creation. Only on that day, when we have no more desires or karma to work out and only wish to be one with God in a state of ecstasy, will we wake from this dream of delusion and enter the highest state of bliss consciousness.

June 1976. I was in Philadelphia about to walk onstage before 120,000 people at John F. Kennedy Stadium. On the bill with me were

Peter Frampton and Yes. My album *The Dream Weaver* had been on the *Billboard* charts since late 1975 and was currently at number 7; in addition, I had two number 2 singles—"Dream Weaver" and, at the time of the concert, "Love Is Alive." It was the largest concert I'd ever played, and the power I felt standing before so many people who were radiating this astounding degree of positive energy was overwhelming. There's no way to accurately describe the emotion I felt as a performer when I began singing "Dream Weaver"—a song I'd written about God's love and compassion—to an audience of that size. In fact, the entire summer was like that—playing at sports stadiums and other huge festivals around the United States and Europe to well over three million people. That summer of 1976 was a life-altering time for me career-wise, the highest point in my life up until then. I was thirty-three and had a lot of questions about who I was and how I would deal with success and my future.

I soon realized that even though I was experiencing a period of great elation, inevitably the highs would wane. I had been moderately successful as a child actor, even playing in a Broadway musical, *Fanny*. From my past experience, having released eleven albums, between my solo records and Spooky Tooth—none of which were commercially successful—I knew the feeling of being pumped up with enthusiasm and then being dropped into despair, despite the star power of the musicians I worked with. I could feel intuitively that this experience of success might give me a great opportunity to test my newly found spiritual path and guru. After all, "Dream Weaver" was a song about God's infinite mercy, carrying us through our trials: "Dream Weaver, I believe you can get me through the night." And trials there were throughout my life. But I never avoided them, I faced them head on, which gave me spiritual muscle. My guru used to say, "A wrestler will never increase his strength unless he works out with a stronger [opponent]."[1] I made God and my guru my best friends early on in my career and car-

ried them with me through all my experiences in life. That changed the entire scope of how I would deal with both success and failure, all the while trying to maintain even-mindedness.

Success does not land in your lap without hard work, something I realized early on in life. Eastern philosophy teaches that qualities and talents are developed and brought over from past lives. You don't just learn to be a genius or acquire any great talent in one lifetime—it takes sustained effort and deep focus to attract success to anything we do.

One

THE BEGINNING

was sixteen years old. It was a late overcast November morning in New Jersey, the streets still wet from rain the night before. I was a junior at Tenafly High School, and two of my closest friends, John McGauley and Eddie Sutton, pulled into my driveway and asked me if I wanted to go for a drive. We had all known each other since the fifth grade and were very close. None of us had driver's licenses. John had borrowed the car—an off-white 1955 Ford—from one of our high school friends who was a senior. This was well before cars were equipped with seat belts, and we were all sitting in the front seat, me at the far right. As we drove up Grant Avenue, where I lived, John was showing off, downshifting while accelerating around a corner and rapidly approaching a concrete bridge over a stream. The road was still wet; the car fishtailed as we made the turn, hit the bridge nearly head on, and then plummeted down the embankment for about ten feet or so. The car ended on its side, almost in the water.

At the moment of impact, I experienced superhuman strength—bracing my knees against the dashboard. Then—complete silence. I

looked over in panic at John and Eddie, but they both looked uncon-
scious. With the car tilted at a precarious angle, I couldn't reach them.
The rear and front windshields had literally blown out of the car on
impact. I lifted my body up over the space where the front windshield
had been and slid down the hood to the ground. The horn was blow-
ing and the tires were still spinning when the tow truck arrived, fol-
lowed by a doctor who rushed down the embankment. I had climbed
up to the street, where cars were beginning to gather. After a few min-
utes, the doctor, looking very serious, told me John and Eddie were
dead.

That I survived the crash with no major wounds or broken bones
was nothing less than a miracle. But the mental anguish was a different
story. I believe this event was the genesis of my spiritual search, a jour-
ney that would take me around the world to experience things I never
dreamed could happen to me and to meet amazing people who would
have a profound cultural impact on the world. Early on I realized how
fleeting life was and how you could be plucked away at any moment
into the mysterious beyond. In India, it is said that life is like a drop of
water trembling on a lotus leaf and may slip away at any moment. My
Catholic upbringing couldn't offer answers to the spiritual questions I
was pondering, and neither could anyone else. It wasn't until years later,
after I had found my spiritual path and my guru, Paramahansa Yoga-
nanda, that I learned that an enlightened master is omniscient, know-
ing all his true devotees who would come to him either in this present
lifetime or in the future. Moreover, such a master has the power to in-
tervene in a devotee's karma and prevent him from harm or even death.
I later realized that it was Yogananda who had intervened in my life at
that moment, sparing me from death so that I could remain here to
carry out my destined role in this incarnation. But there was yet another
part for me to play later on in God's drama.

I was born on April 26, 1943, in Cresskill, New Jersey, a small scenic town and a suburb of New York City about twenty minutes north of the George Washington Bridge. I was the middle child between my older sister, Beverly, and my younger sister, Lorna. My father, Louis Wright, worked for my uncle, who owned a large construction company that built bridges, roads, and various other infrastructure in towns and cities throughout northern New Jersey. My mom, Ann Belvedere, was a housewife and the motivational force behind the family. We lived in a three-story home at 369 Grant Avenue, directly adjacent to a wooded area on the back of our property and my uncle Jim's construction company complex on the west side. Growing up in this rural setting was truly a young boy's dream. Tracking and silently watching the local wildlife in the nearby woods, I knew where many of their burrows and nests were. Much of my time before starting kindergarten was spent playing cowboys and Indians or "army" with my friends who lived down the street. Using some of my uncle's retired heavy equipment—bulldozers, cranes, and the like—we'd create imaginary battles between the good and bad guys. There were private paved roads throughout the construction complex, which as I grew older afforded me the opportunity to drive my go-cart or one of the family cars without breaking the law.

I was entranced by nature as a young boy and especially looked forward to the subtle magic of seasonal change. Autumn particularly inspired me, when the air grew crisp and the green leaves on the oak, beech, and maple trees transformed into a magnificent array of colors as if they'd been painted by some unseen hand. Around Thanksgiving, when the leaves turned brown and fell to the ground, we would rake

them into large piles and dive into them, rolling around in sheer delight. Sometimes we would even set fire to a pile of dry leaves and run through the pungent clouds of smoke as if performing an ancient ritual. (This was, of course, well before such kinds of activities were strictly regulated by the local police and fire departments!) Fall for me was a time of dreaming, reflection, new friends and new beginnings, and the start of a new school year.

Winter soon arrived after Thanksgiving and I anxiously awaited the first snowfall, when everything would become clothed in white and silver. Ice formed on the edges of brooks and streams, and the lakes and ponds would freeze over. Sometimes I'd be up at dawn peering out my second-story bedroom window to see if it had snowed during the night. If it had, I was outside in a matter of minutes dressed for the occasion with snowsuit, galoshes, and woolen gloves. The science of high-tech, cold-resistant clothing materials had not yet arrived; my hands and toes would get numb in the early morning cold and I would have to retreat home to get warm again. One of my favorite activities was looking for animal tracks in the newly fallen snow, usually from rabbits, woodchucks, or raccoons. My goal of course was to follow the tracks until I found their homes, which I did sometimes. I loved nature and its creatures from a very early age, and still do to this day.

Sometimes large winter storms passed through, and if it snowed really hard during the night, my sisters and I would anxiously await the whistle from the police station to blow at eight a.m. sharp, announcing school would be closed that day. That of course meant one thing—riding sleds with our friends all day long. We had so much fun riding down hills in train or airplane formations, or just by ourselves on our American Flyers. If it got too cold, we could always go to a nearby friend's home for hot chocolate and cookies. Some evenings we would go ice skating at our local pond in neighboring Tenafly, and if it was still snowing and the outside lights were on, the experience was breathtaking.

In late February or early March, when it seemed as though winter would never end, slowly the first signs of spring began to emerge. The first buds on trees became visible, or if you looked carefully, you could see the tiny blades of daffodils or tulips peeping through the wintry-hard sleepy ground. Occasionally, an ice storm would pass through during the night and we would wake up to a fantasy spectacle: trees and meadows clothed in a silvery white ice layer, especially dramatic in the shining sun. From a very young age, I wondered at the mystical power that created this subtle magical beauty. I later realized when I became more firmly rooted on my spiritual path that it was "the silent voice of God, ever calling us through the flowers . . . [and] all things that are beautiful."[2]

Summer would finally arrive just after Memorial Day, and our school vacation soon followed. Summer in New Jersey was hot and humid, with the occasional thunder and lightning storm. It also was a time when my friends and I would camp out just with sleeping bags under the stars, staying up late into the night telling ghost stories—one more terrifying than the next. One of our favorite places to camp out was Hank's cabin, a local landmark about halfway up the trail from Cresskill to Alpine. Close to Hank's was a spring where we would pitch camp and cook our food on a campfire. Filling our canteens with the nearby cool spring water or just drinking it with cupped hands was always a high point in our escapades. And of course nothing could taste better to me at that time than bacon and eggs fried over a campfire in the early morning. Years later, in the late sixties, I began meditating and became a vegetarian, but I still remember the delight of those bacon and eggs.

Our family also spent a day sometimes at Pine Lake, where you could have a picnic, swim all day, meet new friends, and keep cool. I was about seven years old when I first learned to swim at Palisades Amusement Park—one of our local attractions—which boasted a huge

saltwater swimming pool. They advertised one weekend that Buster
Crabbe would be giving swimming lessons the following Saturday.
He had won the Olympic gold medal in 1932 for the 400-meter free-
style swimming event before subsequently breaking into acting, where
he played Tarzan, among other roles. There were quite a few kids in
the park that day waiting in the pool to meet him. When it was my
turn, he looked at me and said, "Can you swim?" "No," I answered, "I
came here hoping you'd teach me how." He held out his arms and told
me to kick and paddle. He suddenly dropped his arms, releasing his
support, and there I was—swimming for the first time in this incarna-
tion. I started yelling, "I can swim, I can swim!" half expecting Buster
to start beating his chest with his fists while yelling out the Tarzan war
cry: *"Ah eeh ah eeh ah."* Back at school I could now boast that Tarzan
had taught me how to swim, a huge feather in my cap.

During my early years at Edward H. Bryan Elementary School—
walking distance from our home—I became quite interested in Native
American culture. Cowboys and Indians were very popular among
young boys growing up in the late forties and early fifties, and I loved
reading about the different tribes spread throughout the country: how
they dressed, the kinds of homes they lived in, and their spiritual be-
liefs. I even had several outfits I would wear while playing "cowboys
and Indians" with my friends. We built three tepees in the wooded area
behind our house, where my friends and I would camp out during the
summer. I made the tepees myself, cutting young birch saplings to use
as the frame, then covering them with rolls of burlap I got from my
uncle's construction yard. They looked pretty authentic—from a dis-
tance. I remember receiving a catalogue in the mail featuring Native
American costumes that were available at one store only on the East
Side of New York City. After my relentless badgering, my mom finally
agreed to take me there after school one day. The first thing I saw upon
entering the small store was an authentic Native American headdress

made with real eagle feathers. As payment for my weeding the garden for the next month, my mom agreed to buy it for me. I was thrilled.

The sages of India teach that you start off your present life exactly where you left off in your past life, being reborn into a family, country, time in history, specific socioeconomic status, in wealth or poverty, in good or poor health, all of which will offer you the perfect opportunity to work out your desires and karma that you brought over from the past. On an extremely subtle level, the soul chooses these opportunities knowing what is best for its evolution back home to God. What you don't work out in this life, you are given the opportunity to work out in your next incarnation, or as many lives as are needed until you attain liberation. There is also an integral relationship between karma and astrology. In India, Vedic astrology is considered a very precise science and it takes a highly advanced master to interpret a horoscope correctly. At the moment of your birth, the stars and planets are aligned in such a way to perfectly present you with opportunities for growth and advancement. Picture it as a cosmic obstacle course where some things come easily to us in life and other things are a struggle. The difficult things are the tests we face and personal weaknesses that we must overcome in order to grow and develop strength and spiritual muscle; for ultimately, a life without struggle is an unsuccessful life.

Important, too, are the families we are born into. Many times, they are packaged with unfinished business with our parents or siblings from past incarnations. Both hate and love are powerful attracting forces that draw souls into new families or other close relationships in order to work out karma from the past. Consequently, harboring hate for any individual will inevitably draw you back into a close relationship with that person until you work out and overcome your hatred. As a fast-moving stream smooths out the sharp edges of stones over time, so we as individuals interacting in the close quarters of a family are given the chance to work out unresolved issues carried over from the past.

God designed His cosmic show in such a way so that we could work out all the kinks embedded in our characters—even if it takes many incarnations—until we reach perfection. "This life is a master novel, written by God, and man would go crazy if he tried to understand it by reason alone."[3]

My family had both its challenges and blessings. Dad was over six feet tall and loved sports, especially baseball. He was almost drafted into the minors as a pitcher before he married, but unfortunately he didn't make the final cut. I think at times later on in his life, he regretted not having made it into the minors and then majors; that was his deep unfulfilled desire, which never came to fruition. My dad had his own demons. He never saw his own father, a captain in the Navy, who had been severely wounded during World War I from a fall, which resulted in brain damage. Returning to the United States, he spent the rest of his life in a military hospital for disabled veterans, where he passed away. Dad lived part of his life through me, coming to all my Little League games, especially when I pitched, and cheering me on. Then there was my appearance at a young age in the Broadway musical, *Fanny*, and my stint with the British band Spooky Tooth, which he loved. Once, when I was playing a Spooky Tooth concert at the Whiskey in Hollywood, I spotted my dad sitting at one of the tables near the back, beaming at me in approval—truly a very proud father. He passed on a year later, before my success with "Dream Weaver," succumbing to a lifelong struggle with alcoholism—a very sad loss for me. He never got to see me at the pinnacle of my career.

Dad took pleasure in his work at my uncle's construction company. I think having the know-how to operate heavy machinery like bulldozers, backhoes, and such gave him great satisfaction and, as a boy, I was overjoyed when he'd let me drive them from time to time. We planted a flower and vegetable garden in a large area in back of our house. My job was to make sure it got watered and weeded. That was the start of

my developing a passion for gardening, which is still very much alive in my life. My guru once said, "Humbly serving all with their beauty, flowers say more to us about God than anything else. Each brings a message that the Heavenly Father is right here."[4]

Fishing was high on Dad's list of fun things to do. Every April, when the season began, he and I would drive to one of our favorite streams or reservoirs, hoping to catch trout or bass. I learned a lot about patience during those outings with my father, sitting on the bank of some picturesque lake or stream and silently taking in the beauty around us.

Sometimes during the winter months, we would go ice fishing on one of the large lakes in New York State, rising at four a.m. and driving two hours so we could get a good spot on the ice. On one such occasion, we decided to light a small campfire on the ice near our campsite so we could warm our hands—a big mistake. After about a half hour, I went to check the bait on our fishing gear and then returned to the campfire. Suddenly I heard a loud crunch, and the next thing I knew, I was up to my chest in freezing water. The pain from the icy water stabbed at me like a knife. Dad rushed over and, in a split second, pulled me out—I don't know why he didn't fall in as well. He carried me to our car and turned the heat on full blast. I slowly dried off. Shortly thereafter we returned home, sadly without any fish. In retrospect I intuitively feel yet again that even though I did fall into the lake that wintry morning, a fatal outcome had been mitigated by God through the instrument of my later-to-be guru.

Dad was very handy and was constantly either fixing or building things around the house. He converted our attic into a third-story bedroom for my sister Beverly; built a screened-in porch at the back of our house; created a fieldstone barbeque in our backyard; and turned our basement into a large recreation room where we played music and had parties as we grew into our teens. The biggest venture my father undertook was building a fairly large swimming pool in the backyard, a rare

item at that time in Cresskill. I think that we were probably either the first or second family in our town to have a pool. But we were an unconventional family, with me being on Broadway in *Fanny* and appearing from time to time in various TV drama roles, while my elder sister, Beverly, made regular television appearances on variety shows, singing country and western songs and even yodeling. My regular troop of grammar school friends included John McGauley, Eddie Sutton, and Ricky Spoley, and we spent many warm days and muggy nights swimming in the pool and carrying on late into the night at our home.

As part of our family menagerie, we had chickens, ducks, rabbits, a pig, and even a baby lamb, in addition to dogs and cats. My favorite pet of all was Bucky, the lamb. We acquired him during a trip to a local farm one weekend, where my family regularly purchased fresh vegetables. While my parents were perusing the local fare, I wandered outside and spotted a fenced-in area with a tiny lamb inside. I ran up to the pen and began petting his small black face, daydreaming what it would be like to have a lamb for a pet. My parents must have picked up my feelings as they walked over to the pen, curious about what so entranced me. I pleaded with them to buy the lamb, making all kinds of promises to do extra chores if they'd let me have him. To my great surprise, they consented.

Back at home, Bucky and I had so much fun playing together in the backyard, chasing one another and roughhousing together; he would even buck me at times, but never dangerously. One of his favorite pranks was to untie my shoelaces with his teeth while I was relaxing on our hammock. One summer, several years later, my family had a big party in our backyard. Bucky mingled with the crowd, eating portions of the food guests gave him. The next day I couldn't find him anywhere. I searched and searched, called neighbors, and looked everywhere. Then we got a call that someone had found him dead in one of the fields adjacent to our house. I never knew how he died—probably

something he ate. I was numb with sadness and inconsolable over my loss for many days.

In time, I gradually recovered from the loss, and slowly I turned my interest to our other animals. One of my chores was cleaning out the chicken coop and feeding the chickens every day. Usually, I would collect the eggs very early in the morning and cook them for Dad and myself for breakfast before he went to work. Our chickens were an unusual variety, strangely termed Sex-Linked Cross, and they frequently produced double-, triple-, and even four-yolk eggs. I'll never forget the painful day when I came home from school only to find all our chickens dead. A neighborhood dog—a Dalmatian—had dug a hole under our chicken-wire fence, got into the run, and killed the entire flock. My stomach knotted up as I surveyed the damage—I was devastated.

Having animals from an early age in life taught me a lot about responsibility—and the inevitable pain stemming from attachment to people, animals, and things. I didn't know this intellectually at the time; I only felt it as emptiness and loss—for it's very hard not to be attached to something you love. Yet the very nature of this world is duality: joy and sorrow, love and loss. Our home was a great place for a young boy growing up; from a very early age, I felt a mystical connection with the silent beauty and power of God. "Learn from the loving care with which God has fashioned every living creature that He is . . . a Father of tenderest compassion who treasures each member of His house of earthly life."[5]

Children's personalities usually develop during the first seven years of their lives, according to the sages of India, and many of the traits you see during these early years were brought over from past incarnations. From as far back as I can remember, I loved singing and memorizing all the dialogue from the children's stories I listened to on 78 rpm records like "Bugs Bunny and the Tortoise," "Sip-Sip Supper," and many others. Whenever we went on family summer vacations with long

drives, I would sit in the backseat of our car and reproduce verbatim entire selections from my record collection, singing and acting all the parts of the characters, as well as mimicking all the sound effects—a one-man show. As the traffic and temperature increased, inevitably someone in our family would yell out, "OK, that's enough now," and if I didn't stop, there would be a "Shut up, or I'll go out of my mind!" I had driven the family almost to the edge with my relentless recitations. I must have carried over my desire and ability for singing and acting, and my fascination with sounds and sound effects, from a recent incarnation which later on in my life came into fruition—I was one of the first artists to use synthesizers in modern pop music.

Our mom was born in New York City on November 1, 1912, to Anna and Salvatore Belvedere. Both were born in Palermo, Sicily, and both immigrated to New York during the 1890s. Salvatore—whom we all called Grandpa Charlie—got involved in the wholesale produce business, and the family lived comfortably in a brownstone building in lower Manhattan. The family moved to New Jersey, where Mom excelled in school—graduating high school as the salutatorian of her class. Though she wanted to attend college, her hopes were stifled by the Great Depression. She had no choice but to find work to help the family make ends meet. From an early age, Mom loved music. She had known someone at a local radio station who set up an audition for her and her sister, Josephine. The station manager liked what he heard and hired them to perform regularly, a weekly guest appearance singing duets of the popular songs of the time.

Not far from her home was the popular Rustic Cabin roadhouse in Englewood Cliffs. Well-known bands of the time performed there regularly. My grandfather knew the owner of the venue and one evening paid him a visit with my mom. Before being discovered, Frank Sinatra was a waiter and singer there, and during the course of the evening, the owner (who knew she was a singer) asked my mom to get up and per-

form a duet with Frank and the band. They sang "Night and Day," a popular song of the era. The audience loved it. She signed many autographs that evening. But soon, as she became frustrated with lack of success and not getting the breaks she wanted, she put her singing career aside, marrying our dad in the early thirties and starting a family.

My mother was always very active in community events. She was a Cub Scout mother, a volunteer for the American Legion, and a participant in local stage productions—sometimes with my dad. I remember marching with her and the Cub Scouts down Main Street in Cresskill in several Fourth of July parades. I still have fond recollections from a very early age of her singing a beautiful lullaby, "Mighty Lak'a Rose," while I was falling asleep—a memory deeply embedded in my being to this day. The song was written in the early 1900s and recorded by Bing Crosby in 1945. It was written by Frank L. Stanton and Ethelbert Nevin. I carried out the tradition in my own family, singing that same lullaby to my sons Justin and Dorian when they were babies, as well as more recently to my two granddaughters, Kirra and Aubrey. The lyrics, which she modified slightly, were very soothing and have a special place in my heart:

Sweetest little baby
Everybody knows
Don't know what to call him
But he's mighty lak'a rose
Looking at his Mommy
With eyes so shiny blue
Makes you think that heaven
Is coming close to you

Mom would encourage us to learn songs that we could sing with the entire family at our home or on holidays like Christmas Eve at her

mother's home. A frustrated singer growing up during the Depression, she was unable to realize her career dreams, so she lived them out through her three children. I don't think Mom ever got over not having had her own successful career, and she continually struggled with disappointment, which later on turned into depression. She often told us that she had to work to help support her large family of eight, which was not uncommon during the Depression. Over time, through marriage and motherhood, she sadly watched her dreams recede into the murky pool of unfulfilled desires. She had enormous drive and, at times, was a bit of a stage mother—a character straight out of a Woody Allen movie. She encouraged each of us to learn and develop our skills in both acting and singing. I took lessons in both, as well as classical piano, for about a year. The first piece I learned to play on piano was one of Chopin's polonaises, which I regularly performed at family functions. I loved playing classical pieces on our spinet piano in the living room but hated having to read music. I overcame my dilemma by memorizing the piece I was working on until I no longer needed the sheet music. Then I could just play the piece over and over to my heart's content. My favorites were the Beethoven compositions "Für Elise" and "Moonlight Sonata." To this day, I don't read music—I play everything by ear, whether writing, recording, or performing at live concerts.

Older brothers many times like teasing their younger sisters, and I was no exception. The piano sometimes was the vehicle I used to scare my sister Lorna. I would play Sergei Rachmaninoff's "Prelude in C Sharp Minor" at night in the middle of a loud thunderstorm. Rachmaninoff had huge hands and it was hard to reach all the notes at my age—my hands simply weren't big enough. But I banged it out very loud and that did the trick. If I simply wanted to bother her, I would play a very annoying random pattern until she started screaming at me to stop, and if that didn't work she'd tell my parents. Then I'd stop.

Mom's main focus was on my older sister, Beverly. She not only had

a good voice but could yodel and play the guitar—certainly a novelty in those days. Beverly regularly sang on TV variety shows and acted in various drama series, most notably *I Remember Mama*. She had a steady career performing in supper clubs, cruise lines, and corporate venues throughout the United States and abroad. It was through her connections that I got to see the Beatles perform at their New York debut concert at Carnegie Hall in the early sixties. Later on, I met George Harrison in London and told him I was at the New York show. "You were there?" he asked, astounded. "Yes, but all I could hear was the audience screaming," I answered. This was before sophisticated sound systems were in play.

My first entrance into the business was with my older sister, Beverly, performing on a popular radio drama series named *Grand Central Station*. I was seven years old at the time, several years before the arrival of television. All the actors' performances were live—if you made a mistake, everyone who was listening to the show heard it. I continued to get small parts on several of these kinds of radio shows over the next few years.

Beverly, three years older than I, loved riding horses and being a cowgirl, hence she learned how to yodel at a very young age. We were close and played a lot together with our friends in the forest behind our home or at the baseball field up the street. I think that Beverly inspired me in a subtle way to perform and be fearless before an audience—an attribute that took me quite some time to master. Her talent and showmanship endured even later on in her life when she struggled with her career. Driven by an innate desire to entertain people, she continued to sing and has kept it up to this day out of sheer passion to perform. She still yodels at our family functions!

My sister Lorna was five years younger than I and was the Native American princess of my backyard tribe. In the three tepees on a clearing behind our home, we had great fun dressing up in all our regalia.

Due to our age difference, we weren't that close as brother and sister until after she finished her studies at New York University. We began to spend more time together when she came along with me on several trips to Hawaii during my college years as a tour guide. She is a great cook with an unusual sense of humor, and we became close over the years. Blessed with an amazing voice, she is also an accomplished jazz singer. When I moved to Europe, she visited me several times in England, and when "Dream Weaver" came out and I started touring a lot, I asked her to be one of the backing vocalists.

When I stopped touring in the late 1970s, Lorna signed a deal with Elton John's label, Rocket Records, and released a 1978 album called *Circle of Love*. In the early eighties, she moved to London and released "Police Woman (Queen of the Neon Jungle)," which she wrote and her husband, Adrian Lee, produced. Adrian later on became the keyboardist for Mike and the Mechanics during their run of success in the late 1980s. Lorna also played the onstage role of Vi Petty in *Buddy (The Buddy Holly Story)* in the London West End production. She finally moved back to California a few years ago, to our delight. Adrian, a very talented musician/producer, is a wonderful addition to the family. He is currently active scoring films.

When television did arrive, I got a chance to appear in my first commercial for Post's Sugar Crisp cereal on the *Captain Video and His Video Rangers* show, which was broadcast out of New York. This was live TV. We had several run-throughs before the program began. The set of the commercial was designed to look like a typical suburban kitchen, with a bowl of cereal neatly placed on the table in a breakfast nook. The bowl of Sugar Crisps had been sitting on a table with milk in it under the hot studio lights for several hours and, unbeknownst to me, the milk had turned sour. When the commercial started and I took the first bite, I instantly knew what had happened. I had to muster all the strength of my will not to shriek and spit out the sour milk, pretending instead to

Gary's sister Lorna in 1966

be glad to be eating this delicious new cereal while saying something corny like, "Gee, Mom, this cereal sure tastes good!"

Between the ages of eight and eleven, I went with Mom to New York at least one day a week to "make the rounds" of the various advertising agencies and casting directors. She got their names and contact information from publications similar to *Variety* that were available at the time; she was a good networker. On some of those days, I'd go on auditions, trying out for TV drama parts, commercials, or Broadway shows. I hated having to put on phony smiles or look cute while reciting lines from a script that I had to read cold. Although I fiercely resisted having time taken away from playing baseball—especially Little League, which I was very much into at the time—I see in retrospect how her guidance, tenacity, and persistence were important ingredients

that I acquired and applied later during my career. She helped steer the boat of my own life toward later success, while at the same time fulfilling dreams that circumstances didn't allow her to realize on her own.

My big break as a child actor came just after I turned eleven, when I got the call to go on an audition for a fairly large role in a new Broadway musical, *Fanny*, based on Marcel Pagnol's stories about the owner of a Marseilles bistro and his family. The play was directed by Josh Logan and produced by David Merrick, who during the sixties went on to have a huge career on Broadway producing shows like *Gypsy*, *Hello, Dolly!*, and *Oliver*. In her debut role as an actress on Broadway, Florence Henderson played the part of Fanny, and Ezio Pinza—riding on his huge success in *South Pacific*—played César, the bistro owner. The part I was auditioning for was Césario—Fanny's son and César's grandson. It required both singing and acting skills.

I remember practicing daily with a vocal coach named Mrs. Harrington, who taught me the song "The Happy Wanderer," the composition Mom and I chose for me to sing for the audition. The first audition went well—even though I was very nervous singing and acting in front of Josh Logan—a true genius of the stage at the time. Before *Fanny*, he had already directed *South Pacific*—which he cowrote with Rodgers and Hammerstein—as well as *Annie Get Your Gun* and *Mister Roberts*. After several callbacks, we got the call that I made the cut—not for Césario, but for his understudy.

Crestfallen, I accepted the offer, even though it was not the role I'd been preparing for. After all, being in a successful Broadway musical at that time was a major stepping-stone in my life that opened many doors and prepared me for my future. When the show opened, I played a minor role as an altar boy, while mentally rehearsing the role of Césario in anticipation of playing it one day. Sure enough, about ten months later my chance arrived when Lloyd Reese, the young actor playing the role at the time, decided to quit. I was asked to take over the part.

When Mom got the call, I remember how the whole family started jumping up and down in sheer delight after she told us the good news! For the next two years, I performed as Césario nightly, soaking up the laughs and applause from the audiences. It was certainly quite a lot for a young boy to take in and not become an egotistical brat in the process. I think that staying in a public school in the suburbs of New Jersey, rather than going to a professional school for child actors, had a lot to do with my staying "normal." Having met some of those kids in the past, I inwardly vowed never to develop the kind of personality that would be repugnant to me and contrary to my deepest values. I also think latent spiritual inclinations were coming into play, guiding me. We had had several family conversations about my going to professional school in New York, and each time we all unanimously agreed that staying in the Cresskill elementary school system was the correct choice.

During the run of the show, I also appeared with Florence Henderson on Ed Sullivan's *Toast of the Town*, better known as *The Ed Sullivan Show*, singing the duet we performed nightly in *Fanny*—"Be Kind to Your Parents." The show was perhaps the most widely viewed program at that time and I was very nervous at the thought of singing before millions of people—live TV again. But after we finished singing the song, Ed remarked, "That Gary Wright is a fine little performer" as we exited the stage. I thought it was very kind of him to say that about me.

Acting with stage legends of the time in front of sold-out audiences, singing with the accompaniment of a full orchestra, these experiences were subtle but deep influences in my life that shaped my skills as a writer, singer, and performer. In retrospect, I see that the Divine Stage Manager once again was molding my life for His plans for me in the not so distant future.

Being on Broadway taught me a lot about life at a very young and

impressionable age. Initially, one of my parents would drive me to New York for the performances, but that was hard for my dad because he had to get up early for work and we never got home before midnight. The problem was solved by another member of the cast, Henry Michel, who was Ezio Pinza's understudy in the show. Henry lived near us in New Jersey and offered to take me with him on the nightly journey to the city. We talked about sports, acting, and his frustrations with the business and getting the big roles. He even gave me advice on my performances, which he observed from the wings while I was onstage. *Fanny* played at the Majestic Theatre and we commuted there by subway, which was kind of scary for me as an eleven-year-old—especially at night, when we had to walk from the subway station to his car in a not-so-desirable area. He seemed to be in tune with my apprehensions, giving me a reassuring hug. Henry was like a father to me and I shall never forget him.

Wednesdays and Saturdays were matinee days and I got to eat dinner between shows at various theater district restaurants in Manhattan, with different members of the cast. I'll never forget my first experience of having Indian food with one of the actors in the show. The smell of the spices, the aromas from the various dishes, left a deep impression on me—probably having awakened a past-life memory. There was a lot of free time at night before the show actually started, and I would use it to listen to music on the small radio I had in my dressing room. My real passion at the time was early rhythm and blues and, later on, rock and roll. Little Richard, Fats Domino, Ray Charles, and many other doo-wop groups were my favorites. Between shows on matinee days, I spent hours at Colony Records on Broadway buying 45s of my favorite songs, usually aired on the Alan Freed show. I fell in love with music but didn't know you could make a living at it.

Just after turning twelve, I had a serious talk with my parents and told them I had decided to leave *Fanny* and return to a "normal" life.

They knew I was burned out performing the same role every night for almost two years and, in full support of my decision, gave me their blessing. Intuitively, I realized that acting wasn't my calling. It seemed too insecure as a profession, and though I got many calls to be in other Broadway shows with big parts, I turned them all down with the exception of the occasional TV commercial or a one-off drama TV acting part. I would accept these to help pay for my future college education. Growing up in suburbia, I so wanted to return to life as it was before Broadway—hanging out with my friends, playing Little League baseball, camping out—all those things important to a boy my age that I felt I had missed out on.

Junior high at Edward H. Bryant in Cresskill came with both fun and emotional tests. Music became a passion in my life, and my collection of 45 rpm records was huge. I even started singing informally in local doo-wop groups, usually rehearsing in the front of drugstores that had a passageway before the entrance, which offered a lot of natural reverb when we sang. I had the hairdo and some very cool clothes that I had bought on 42nd Street near the neighborhood I frequently visited while in *Fanny*. Elvis, Jerry Lee Lewis, and Carl Perkins had just emerged on the music scene, and I remember spending hours on the piano with my record player next to me trying to figure out what Jerry Lee was playing on "Whole Lotta Shakin' Goin' On." I finally learned it and felt a sense of victory as I played along with Jerry Lee—without any sheet music. I couldn't figure out how he did the glissandos without totally destroying his fingernails, but I came up with a very practical solution—liquid furniture polish applied over the entire keyboard did the trick! From that time on, anything I learned from a record was achieved by ear only.

Life at home unfortunately was becoming dysfunctional. My father had developed a drinking problem that began when I was younger and was now getting worse. My mom, who had been the strength in the

family all those years, began exhibiting symptoms of bipolar disorder, although we didn't know what that was at the time. Psychology was still a very young field. Moreover, you never told anyone you were seeing a psychiatrist for fear of being ostracized and, even worse—crazy. In retrospect, experiencing firsthand what it was like growing up with a bipolar mother became the impetus for my wanting to study psychology later on in college. My goal was to get a degree in psychology, go to med school, and then do my residency in psychiatry—trying subconsciously to fix a problem in the family that at the time couldn't be fixed. We all thought that she was just getting more aggressive and pushy, not realizing that there was a chemical imbalance in her body. There weren't a lot of treatment choices at that time, and so she progressively got worse. I began feeling emotionally abandoned as time passed and family life deteriorated. Detaching myself from the situation as best as I could, and often reminding myself that I soon would be eighteen and on my own, I stayed positive and drew great support from close friends. During that time, I practiced what the yogis call *titiksha*—mental opposition to negative states of consciousness—though I didn't know such a remedy existed at the time. I managed to get through junior high and then high school, excelling in basketball, baseball, and, of course—music.

Indian philosophy teaches that the families we attract into our lives are the precise vehicles we each need in order to overcome our character liabilities brought over from the past. Substance abuse and mental instability was difficult for me to understand. Later on in my life I often asked myself why I had attracted this. How could I grow through this experience? But as I grew older, all I could do was forgive my parents—for they were doing the best they could under the circumstances and conditions that they brought over from their past. Moreover, I gradually realized that carrying resentment and anger with me all my life would only produce one thing—the fruit of bitterness, which I chose not to

drag along with me. Forgiveness is the higher road. Forgiveness is powerful. In India, it is said that the universe continues to exist only through continual forgiveness.

There was no high school in Cresskill at that time. All of us who attended grammar school and junior high at Edward H. Bryant school went to neighboring Tenafly High, which was highly rated academically. Word got around that Ricky Nelson's cousin, Willy, went to Tenafly High as well. My newly acquired friend Bill Markle introduced me to Willy, and we talked about starting a band together with Charlie Leahy, which became Willy Nelson and the Dukes (not to be confused with country icon Willie Nelson). We played at various school events like sock hops and dances, playing popular tunes of the time, including some of Ricky Nelson's hits. Bill played guitar, Charlie was on drums, Willy was the front man, and I was on keyboards. Bill and I left the Dukes and recruited another new friend, Vic Losick, to play drums in our newly formed trio. I still had my furniture polish for the Jerry Lee Lewis tunes we performed. I loved playing in a band, but despite having been on Broadway, I was shy when it came to speaking to an audience, something I think I brought over from the past. It started when I was in *Fanny* and I took over the role of Césario. I was terrified that I would forget my lines and couldn't get rid of the fear. One night I actually did stumble over a fairly large passage, and the stage manager had to yell out the lines from the wings. I was petrified and he scolded me after the curtain call, which made it even worse. It never happened again, thank God, but I wasn't completely healed. I still carried around a deep fear of embarrassment, of making a fool of myself. Even when my career took off later on, it was a year or so before I became totally comfortable speaking to both small and large

audiences. I realized then that I had finally overcome that fear in this incarnation.

We had no bass player, but that was OK because in those days not a lot of people played bass—especially in high school bands. Ironically, during the course of my career I seemed to always have had issues with bass players and the parts they chose to play. I heard and still hear my music a certain way, and many of my songs revolve around a specific bass part that I play on keyboard when I'm writing a song. Consequently, I wound up playing keyboard bass on all my records, with the exception of a few tracks, starting with *The Dream Weaver* album. I played in various combinations of different bands throughout high school, one of which was The Impalas, adding second guitarist George Miller and a new drummer, Steve Schatzberg. We would rehearse in my living room while my father read the newspaper sitting in his easy chair in the middle of all the amps and drums. None of us had driver's licenses and usually my dad or Bill's brother, Gil, would drive us to the venues. On the odd occasion, however, we would "borrow" one of my uncle's pickup trucks from the construction company—sneaking in at dusk and moving a bulldozer to get to the truck. We loaded the gear into the truck, went to the show, played, and returned home without being found out.

During that period, Bill Markle and I made some recordings under the name "Gary and Billy." "Lisa, Lisa" was the first single we released, and it was played on *American Bandstand*, with good audience response. I remember that afternoon. Bill and I were over at his girlfriend Alice Sutton's house watching the show on TV, when host Dick Clark announced our song. Suddenly, life went into slow motion as we watched couples dance to our music! It was a surreal experience, hearing your song on TV at such an impressionable age. The next day at school, we were treated like gods by our friends. Everyone wanted to know what it felt like to hear your song on the most popular music show on TV at the

time. Bill and I remained on cloud nine for most of the day. "Lisa, Lisa" never became a hit, and in my senior year in high school, I started yet another group, The Coachmen Five. We played at various clubs at the Jersey shore, as well as Lake George, New York, during our summer break. The lineup was Frank Zillito on guitar, Jimmy Carrol or Eddie Brick on vocals, Steve Bogue on drums, me on keyboards and vocals, and finally a bass player, Billy Osmolski. It was a really fun time in my life, getting out and doing what I really liked—playing and singing. My tastes were still heavily in R&B, although we still performed Beatle songs and other popular instrumentals and contemporary hits.

My high school classes were geared toward getting accepted into a good college. My favorite class was honors English with an inspiring teacher named Horatio Wirtz, who taught me a lot about writing. I was the senior editor of our yearbook and a member of the track team—though I didn't do very well in pole vaulting. Graduating with honors, I got accepted to the College of William and Mary in historic Williamsburg, Va. The campus and town were beautiful, but soon their charm wore off. I missed the big-city life and being close to New York. Mid-sophomore year, I transferred to New York University, where I received my degree in psychology. NYU was a very good school academically, but there wasn't a lot of social life on campus, as there had been at William and Mary. Consequently, I buried myself in my studies; my social life was playing with The Coachmen Five whenever I could, which was a good balance for me. I was now financing my entire college education alone, through work and scholarships, and had to maintain a high grade point average, both to keep my scholarships and to get into medical school.

I eventually left The Coachmen Five and joined forces with a great local saxophone player named Billy Crandall, who had been in The Royal Teens along with the very young, yet-to-be Four Seasons producer Bob Gaudio. The Royal Teens delivered the hit "Short Shorts."

Billy was the closest thing stylistically to King Curtis—my favorite sax player by far—and he lived just down the street from me. Billy changed his name to Buddy Randell, and the new band was called The Twist-abouts, with Buddy on sax and vocals, Bill Markle on guitar, Bobby Palen on drums, Bill Elmiger on bass, and me on lead vocals and Hammond organ. Later on in 1965, Buddy formed a group called The Knickerbockers, which had a hit with the song "Lies." Playing during the summer breaks with The Twistabouts taught me a lot about differ-ent styles of music that I hadn't been exposed to, and as we played more and more, the band became really tight.

I realized at the end of my junior year at NYU that I had to shift gears financially in order to complete my undergraduate studies and have enough for med school. I was virtually on my own financially at this stage in my life. Working in the band just wasn't bringing in enough money to sustain me. My friend Bill's older brother, Gil, had just found a great job as a tour conductor taking groups to Europe during the summer months while he attended Yale. Intuitively, I felt that was something I could do as well. I began scouring the yellow pages of the Manhattan phone book, calling just about every travel agency listed. After almost giving up, I got a positive response from one of the last calls I made to a company named Male Travel Inc., which was starting to take groups to Hawaii on charter flights. The trips lasted two weeks, with three days in Los Angeles, a week in Oahu, and three days in San Francisco. The company was looking for tour guides. I met with the owner of the company—a Frenchman named René Pouteau—and got the job. I could hardly believe it: being paid to travel to great places like Hawaii, which at that time was still very unspoiled—there were only a dozen or so hotels in Waikiki Beach in 1964 and only two on Maui.

The people I worked with were wonderful and supportive. More-over, the money I would be receiving, between salary and tips, was enough to cover my last two years in college and first year of med school. Years later, I read something my guru said about tenacity: You need to turn over all the stones until you find what you're looking for without losing hope in the process, knowing that God is guiding you toward the fulfillment of all worthy goals.

During my trips to Hawaii in the early 1960s, I became drawn to the writings of Hermann Hesse. Free time during the days while on Oahu allowed me to visit one of the beautiful beaches near our hotel to read *Siddhartha*—one of his books that attracted me at the time. I finished the book on an Easter Sunday morning while on the beach, and still re-member the feelings of connection and being part of everything around me—my first spiritual experience. I had never read anything before about finding enlightenment or traveling the road of self-discovery; I was fascinated by the concept of Nirvana and being able to go into states of ecstasy. Later on, I realized that God is manifest in beauty; feeling His presence in the flowers, the clouds, the breeze, and the ocean was easier to experience in a place like Hawaii. A door had opened for me and I was eager to see what was beyond.

I was attracted to *Siddhartha* because the book both answered ques-tions and challenged my early religious beliefs. As mentioned earlier, I was raised in the Catholic faith and attended Mass with my family regularly while living in New Jersey. I always admired the devotion that several members of the congregation demonstrated during Mass or on religious holidays. Receiving First Communion when I was about eight years old made me feel really special at the time, and I always looked forward to going to confession and receiving Holy Communion on Sundays or during special holidays—a devotional part of me that was longing to express itself. Yet I had trouble accepting the doctrines that proclaimed eternal hellfire for sinners or how perfect one would have to

be to get to heaven. I knew *something* was there, but I didn't know what it was or how to incorporate it into my being. During my adolescence, I decided not to receive Confirmation and more or less abandoned Catholicism—but not my spiritual path, which developed later.

My long-term career goal from the time I entered college was to become a doctor—specifically, a psychiatrist. At that time in my life, I wanted something substantial that offered security—certainly not music, because one couldn't make a living as a musician, or at least that's what I thought at the time. I took all the necessary classes in pre-med during my undergraduate years and graduated from NYU in 1965. I applied to several medical schools during my senior year and chose Downstate Medical College in Brooklyn, which was connected with Kings County Hospital. I had no idea how grueling the first year of medical school would be, sleeping four or five hours a night and attending classes or studying for exams the rest of the time.

From time to time, I would leave Brooklyn and take the subway to Manhattan to sit in on a recording session produced by Jimmy Miller and Larry Fallon—two friends of the family. Jimmy was a drummer and Larry a piano player, and they occasionally played with my sister Beverly when she did club dates in the area. Jimmy had a great sense of humor and was larger than life and fun to be around—the perfect relief I needed from my stressful studies. At the time, Jimmy and Larry were producing mainly R&B singles for various record labels and always had the best New York session players. Making those excursions was nourishment for my soul because it allowed me to reconnect to music again before I had to return to the medical grindstone.

I had always done well in my studies while at NYU, but med school was a different story. I was consumed by the experience, and to make matters worse I was doing poorly on my exams. They were full of tricky multiple choice questions and you had to have an absolutely precise knowledge of the topic to give the correct answer. I failed to pass the

final exams, and at the end of the year my goal of being a doctor suddenly and dramatically evaporated into thin air. I'll never forget the drive home after I got the news of not passing—I was numb and very confused: five years of studying down the drain. Both my parents were very sympathetic, and that gave me comfort.

I quickly decided to go abroad and continue my studies in postgraduate psychology. Having visited Italy and Greece while I was in college, I wanted to return and live somewhere in Europe where I could be part of a culture that inspired me both aesthetically and intellectually. I applied to several universities and was accepted to the Freie University of Berlin—right after the wall had been erected and right in the middle of Communist East Germany. I did several more tours for Male Travel and saved up enough to finance my adventure. I felt somehow I was being guided by a subtle spiritual power and that the decision was the right one. In September 1966, I boarded a Pan Am flight to Berlin, closing one chapter of my life and opening another—the seeds of my karma were blossoming into events I never in my wildest dreams thought could happen to me.

MY PATH EMERGES

My choice of Berlin and the Freie University was a practical decision. I had studied German for three years as an undergraduate, mainly because German was considered a scientific language and possibly useful in the future if I were to pursue medical research. In high school, I had studied Spanish for three years, but the thought of studying postgraduate psychology in Spain didn't feel right, first because my German was much better than my Spanish, and second because much of psychology had its origins in Germany and Switzerland. Languages had always come easily to me, probably because of my ability to sing and mimic sounds. The grammar part of the equation was another story, but slowly I became proficient in the language.

When I first arrived in Berlin, I didn't know anyone or where to stay; my fumbling German made the situation even more frustrating. Another tour guide from Male Travel had given me the phone number of an acquaintance of his, a dentist living in Berlin. I called him from a pay phone—the kind you had to keep dropping in coins or be disconnected—and was trying to explain my situation to him over the crackling phone line. After a couple minutes of shouting back and

forth, I finally figured out what he was trying to tell me: his dad had passed away only minutes before my phone call! I felt so foolish at having inadvertently bungled my way into his life at such a very private and profound moment. I gave him my condolences while trying at the same time to be comforting, and hung up.

That evening, I found a reasonable hotel, where I spent my first few days while looking for a room to rent through an agency. In the past, I had rented rooms while doing my undergraduate work in New York, but this was a totally different experience. I quickly became very impressed with German efficiency and practicality when dealing with basics like finding a place to live. After looking at several places in different parts of the city, I found a large room on the second floor of a large apartment in Charlottenburg—a very fashionable and charming part of the city. Owners Herr and Frau Lange resided there with their daughter and grandson. My room had a high ceiling and a large bay window looking down to Wielandstrasse. The room came with breakfast—typically freshly baked bread rolls from the bakery down the street, two boiled eggs, butter, marmalade, and that great dark German coffee. There was an alcove next to the bay window where sunlight poured into the room and where I had my breakfast and sometimes lunch each day while adjusting to my new name—Herr Wright.

While enrolling at the Freie University, I met a few Americans who were studying there as well. As all my classes would be in German, someone suggested that I should enroll at the Goethe-Institut, a nonprofit organization promoting the German language and culture, and take a crash course in the language. Three years of college German had taught me a lot, but I needed to speak it and own it in order to excel. I enrolled in a three-month program, working around my classes at the university. Slowly I began to master the language; finally a big breakthrough came when I had my first dream in German—a sign that one is rapidly progressing in a language. There was no real opportunity or

necessity to speak English anymore, since all the people I dealt with spoke German, with the exception of the few Americans I met when I initially enrolled. My classes at the university were challenging at first, as they were all in German, but I gradually immersed myself in the language, art, and culture, and things began brightening up for me. The European university system is different from the American system in that an American bachelor's degree is equivalent only to the first two years at a European university. Consequently, being enrolled as a post-graduate student in psychology meant that I had to retake several basic courses like statistics all over again. I sailed through them, having already taken them at NYU, but it felt like a waste of time to me.

Gary near his apartment in Berlin, Germany, where he lived while doing postgraduate work in psychology at Freie University of Berlin.

I started hanging out at various coffee bars and began meeting people, some of whom turned out to be duds. It's hard to assess someone's character when you haven't completely mastered the subtle nuances of a new language, but I tried as best as I could. First impressions are very important. If you want to know about a person when you first meet, look deeply into their eyes—the windows of the soul—and simultaneously feel in your heart the vibrations you are receiving from that individual. You will then know if they are a friend from the past or someone undesirable that you should avoid. I wish I had had that wisdom earlier.

One individual in particular had a role to play in my life. I met him at a chic local hangout on Kurfürstendamm called Drugstore, a fashionable area of Berlin near my apartment. Now, Berlin in 1966 was surrounded by the newly erected Berlin Wall, and Drugstore was one of those places where you could imagine spies or intelligence agents trading secrets or doing deals under the table. Dirk and I met one late afternoon over coffee and I think he was fascinated by my being an American living in Berlin and speaking German. He started inviting me to go to clubs with him to check out the music scene and nightlife in the city. It was quite fascinating for me because I soon realized that people took club-going very seriously, dressing to the nines and looking very cool—even surrealistic. Thick, over-the-top makeup; long fur coats; and matching hats were sometimes punctuated by thigh-high boots. This was the time when men wore their hair long, grew beards, and maybe even wore makeup themselves. Occasionally, someone would arrive wearing a long velvet cape with high boots and a ruffled shirt, looking like a prince. You could smell patchouli and other scented oils everywhere. Women wore their hair long with hair bands and donned hippie dresses.

Some clubs were happening from nine p.m. till around midnight; others just started happening around midnight and lasted until about three a.m.; and last were those that only happened from about three

a.m. till dawn, where the real creatures of the night emerged. This was all very new to me and, along with the great mix of music I was being exposed to, I began to feel that I wanted to embrace this culture and be more a part of it. In 1966, the "British Invasion" of music and culture was spreading all over Europe, along with flower power, psychedelic drugs, and rebellion against the status quo.

Consequently, I spent a lot of late evenings at clubs listening to great music. It was actually a blessing in disguise that I was taking classes that I had already passed back in the States; otherwise I would have never had the time to explore the music scene as I did. I'll never forget the first time I heard "Gimme Some Lovin'" by The Spencer Davis Group, sung by Steve Winwood. It left a major impression on me. The production was unusual and amazing for its time. The tribal feeling of the track, especially the simple but driving bass line, and the overdriven Hammond organ with the simple but great part Steve played brought everyone to the dance floor. Then sixteen-year-old Steve's vocal came in, and the whole track shifted gears to a higher level—an emotional crescendo. It was probably one of the most soulful vocal performances I'd ever heard, especially with my background in R&B. But the big surprise didn't come till later on, when I learned that Jimmy Miller, my friend from New Jersey, was the producer of the track. Frustrated with not playing in a band, I bought a nylon-string guitar and began taking flamenco guitar lessons, which I really enjoyed. I spent many hours sitting in the sunlit alcove of my room playing my guitar. Slowly the bud of my love for music began to open again, though I tried to resist it with my academic logic of wanting to get my Ph.D. in psychology.

To make life a bit easier, I bought a VW bug so I could drive to the campus from my room in Charlottenburg and not have to take the S-Bahn and subway. I befriended another student, Mayo, from the university and she took me several times into East Berlin to attend student parties at Humboldt University. Mayo had a West German passport,

and along with my American passport, we could both freely enter and leave without any major problems. The parties we attended were fascinating for me, since all the students were from the Eastern Bloc countries, China, or Cuba—people I'd never met before. It was a given for students not to talk politics, for fear of being turned in and interrogated by the dreaded Stasi secret police force. My experience of being in the East was of always feeling that undercurrent of paranoia wherever I went. The shops had long lines and very meager supplies; the radio stations regularly pumped out East German (DDR) propaganda denouncing the West; and there were virtually no lights lighting up East Berlin at night. With few exceptions, people looked pretty grim most of the time.

Going from vibrant West Berlin into the Eastern Zone was like watching an HD color movie turn into black and white, and visiting the newly erected Berlin Wall was depressing. If a tourist happened to stray a little too close to one of the security towers, the border guards inside would immediately focus their binoculars on them. Routinely they would flash their rifles, indicating their readiness to shoot anyone who dared to enter "no-man's-land," a strip of land between the two heavily fortified walls, also known as the "death strip." The East German border security force would mainly use non–East Germans from the Eastern Bloc countries as border guards. The reasoning was that nonnatives would be more likely to shoot fleeing East Germans than their own countrymen. One experience that stands out in my memory is a May Day celebration in the East, comparable to an American Fourth of July parade but at the same time worlds apart: the East German army marched in goose-step synchronicity, with various other worker groups following behind, including airline employees, auto workers, bakers, and the like. Marching in the parade was compulsory. Red flags hung down from windows on the upper stories of buildings, and the event closed with a chilling speech by head of the German Democratic

Republic, or East Germany, Walter Ulbricht, punctuated by crowds raising their clenched fists and shouting something like "Hail." It was the closest thing to what I would have imagined a Nazi rally to be.

That period in Berlin was a time of soul searching, and I was becoming more and more frustrated being a postgraduate student at the university. Moreover, the prospect of spending many more years in a German university to get my doctorate was rapidly losing its appeal. I felt I needed a break from my studies so I could figure out what I wanted to do with my life. After all, I had been in college, med, and postgraduate school for nearly six years straight. An urge was gnawing at my psyche to go out and play music like I had done back in the States while in college. I made an agreement with myself that this was to be only a break from my studies, and not a permanent career move. That decision would be made later on after I had had a little fun doing what I loved.

I hadn't heard of any American bands touring around Germany and thought the concept might be appealing to local promoters and agents. A plan began to emerge, and I began to contact musicians I had known back in New Jersey, including Jimmy Carrol from The Coachmen Five. The response from everyone I contacted was overwhelmingly positive, as none of them had ever been to Europe. The first hurdle I needed to overcome was finding someone to finance bringing the musicians and equipment over to Berlin. A thought flashed in my mind to contact Rita Lynn, my German friend Dirk's former landlady. She had always been interested in my stage and musical background and had the financial wherewithal to help out. I mapped out my plan to her, and she agreed to underwrite the venture. I realized that I had to shore up my own personal finances in order to live for an unknown period of time, so I got on the phone to Male Travel and let them know I was available to do tours again.

I contacted the Freie University and told them I would not be re-

turning for the next semester, which was about to begin in February. Rita and I met one last time to go over plans—especially the costly shipping of my cumbersome Hammond organ, which would be a necessary and musically vital part of my new band. Herr and Frau Lange were very disappointed to lose their American tenant, who had become a part of their family. I took a last look at my room overlooking Wieland-strasse, where I had studied, planned, dreamed, and played flamenco guitar. Bidding farewell to my German friends, I turned a page and closed a stormy chapter of my life.

I called Male Travel upon my arrival in New York and got on a tour to Hawaii a week later. The warm tropical sunshine in February felt wonderful after the cold winter I had spent in Berlin, and I began to read Hermann Hesse again. I was also becoming interested in Hawaiian spiritually and spent many evenings with local friends listening to stories about the healing powers of the Hawaiian medicine men—the kahunas. My thirst for spiritual knowledge and direction was growing.

In between tours, I held auditions at home in Cresskill, where I was temporarily living. After quite a few auditions, I decided to take a guitar player, a drummer, and Jimmy Carrol. I would play bass on the Hammond organ foot pedals, and Jimmy and I would share the lead vocals. We began rehearsing our material, mainly Ray Charles, James Brown, the Beatles, and several more R&B songs popular at the time. After much deliberation, I came up with the name "The New York Tymes" and made final arrangements to have the amps, organ, and drums shipped overseas. In the late spring of 1967, we all arrived in Berlin. Rita had found a place for us to rehearse at a club called Drafi's near the East German border. The club was named after the German pop star Drafi Deutscher, who would make an appearance every now and then to greet guests. I think he liked our music since, as a touring American soul band, we were a novelty in Germany at that time. I remember Drafi sitting at a table in the back of the club, rocking back

and forth and cheering us on. He was born in Berlin and was best known for his 1965 hit *"Marmor, Stein und Eisen Bricht,"* which was a huge success, selling more than one million copies and garnering him a gold record. When we met him, he was going through a tough time in his career, but he rebounded in the eighties with his new duo, Mixed Emotions. During our daytime rehearsals, agents and promoters began dropping by to check us out. As our rehearsals progressed, I saw that playing foot pedals on the Hammond organ and singing at the same time was too complicated for me, so I decided to find a bass player.

Gary's band "The New York Tymes" in Berlin, Germany, circa 1966.

After several auditions, we hired Peter Blaar, an experienced bass player and Berlin native. Peter had a good handle on the German club scene, and his practical experience proved invaluable over the next few months: when it came to driving the German autobahns, navigating German cities (with only a city map if there was one), dealing with promoters, or advising us which were the coolest clubs, Peter was our

man. Opening night at Drafi's had its challenges, but we got through it and regrouped the next few days, perfecting the show. After a two-week engagement in Berlin, an agent Rita had found booked us a club tour of Germany. I was excited because my past playing experiences were limited to New Jersey and New York, but now my first European tour was about to unfold. I was glad to leave the confinement of Berlin to see other parts of West Germany. As we played clubs in different cities and U.S. military bases, we began to receive positive responses from the audiences and promoters. Germans are known to be very passionate about their music, as were the soldiers on the American military bases, which made performing even more rewarding. I was having a blast doing what I loved—and getting paid for it; not a lot, but enough to live on.

During this period, on our long drives between venues, I began listening more and more to music coming out of the U.K., like the Jimi Hendrix Experience, Cream, Traffic, and Pink Floyd. We would usually listen to either Radio Caroline or Radio Luxembourg, both of which were the equivalent of early FM radio stations in the States. But the album that deeply moved me and that I couldn't stop playing was the Beatles' *Sgt. Pepper's Lonely Hearts Club Band*. I was blown away by the quality of songwriting, musicianship, and singing. I had always liked their music in the past, but this album was different. One of the tracks I played over and over was George Harrison's "Within You Without You." It somehow struck a chord in me, with its use of Indian instruments, the unusual lyrics, and overall arrangement. I first heard the song sitting in the back of the van that we traveled in. I was wearing headphones, and when the intro came in with the sitar, tamboura, and the tablas, I was transported to another plane of consciousness. I'd never heard such sound textures before. It was a preview from the Divine Friend of someone I was to meet in the future who would have a deep influence over me.

From a cultural point of view, the sixties in European cities were something very new and fascinating for me. Having grown up on the U.S. East Coast during the fifties and early sixties, I was seldom exposed to an environment that was so culturally and artistically appealing. After all, I was only used to living in Berlin, which was truly unto itself; but traveling through the rest of Germany as well as Switzerland, Holland, and Scandinavia, really began to inspire me creatively. The music I heard on the radio, the clothes in the quaint little boutiques, the restaurants, the clubs and museums all became ambrosia I feasted on daily. Clothes were a big part of my life started during this period. I began to create the persona of who I wanted to be and what that would look like.

While at a gig in Hamburg, I met a musician from another working band who mentioned that they had just toured Norway and how much fun they had had. He gave me the name and contact information of a Norwegian promoter named Barry. I contacted him, and after a long conversation, he invited The New York Tymes to do a small tour of Norway. After finishing our engagements in northern Germany, we drove to the nearest port and then took the ferry to the capital city of Oslo. It was late summer in 1967, and the Nordic landscape was breathtaking as we arrived in the harbor. The air was crisp and the gentle breeze seemed to be playing with the occasional white clouds that passed by. The seawater was very clean, as was the city itself, with its picturesque stone bridges connecting canals to main thoroughfares. Initially we began playing clubs in and around Oslo, but we also played at some very unusual venues.

I remember at times driving down a two-lane road in the middle of a beautiful pine forest and then turning onto a dirt road and driving about five or ten miles through a Hansel-and-Gretel-like wooded area that ended in a large field. In the middle of an open area was a large gazebo where the band was supposed to set up on a small stage raised

above the dance area. The first time this happened, I was sure this couldn't be the venue because of its remoteness—but it was. One by one, cars began to arrive, along with a food van, which parked near the stage. As we played into the night, I began observing a rather peculiar cultural characteristic of the Norwegians. While couples were dancing, they would occasionally bump into each other without excusing themselves. I thought this was odd but they seemed to be having fun and didn't think they were at all being rude. That's one of the challenging parts of traveling around the world—learning the cultural differences between countries and accepting them without being judgmental, and seeing all as part of God's large family.

In early September, Barry called me and asked if we would be interested in opening for Traffic at a fairly large theater in Oslo. It was Traffic's first show of a European tour they were embarking on to promote their first album, *Mr. Fantasy*. The band consisted of Steve Winwood, Chris Wood, Jim Capaldi, and Dave Mason. Their manager, and Island Records founder, Chris Blackwell was at the venue and I introduced myself to him. We had a common friend in Jimmy Miller, whom Chris had hired to produce for his new label. Jimmy had already produced the first two big singles for Chris with The Spencer Davis Group—"Gimme Some Lovin'" and "I'm a Man." Steve Winwood, its lead singer, had left shortly thereafter to form Traffic.

I was a big fan of Steve's voice and admired his great talent as a musician as well. As I waited with Chris on the side of the stage for Traffic to emerge, I had a flashback of the first time I heard "Gimme Some Lovin'" at the club in Berlin and how impressed I was. As the band sauntered onto the stage and began to play, I was blown away. In addition to Steve's great vocals, keyboard and guitar playing were the band's overall musical talent. I was also impressed with Dave Mason's performance of "Hole in My Shoe," which was their first single. Seeing Dave playing the sitar on the song was an eye-opener for me; it was an instru-

ment I'd only heard on *Sgt. Pepper's* but never seen being played live before, perhaps another preview of something I would hear a lot more of in the future.

Unbeknownst to me, Chris had seen my band perform in the earlier part of the show. When the concert was over, he came up to me and told me how he liked my voice and asked me if we would be interested in coming to London to record for his new label, Island Records. I couldn't believe what I was hearing; taking a leap from playing in clubs to recording for a cutting-edge label in London was hard to absorb. "Of course we'll come to London," I told him. We agreed to arrive in October, only a few weeks away. My plans of returning to postgraduate school seemed to be more and more remote. This was the real thing; and even better, Jimmy Miller would be producing us.

I had never really seriously written a song before, but now I had to start almost immediately. Writing on the Hammond organ was out of the question because for practical reasons it remained in our trailer with the drums and our other gear. Moreover, it was far too bulky to move into our individual hotel rooms that we occupied. But I still had my nylon-string acoustic guitar with me that I had bought in Berlin, the one I had taken flamenco lessons on. I began playing different chord patterns until an idea emerged that I found extremely compelling. I had a title floating in my head, "Sunshine Help Me," which I sensed would marry well with my chord changes. The verse melody I wrote was more blues/rock than R&B, and the song built in the pre-chorus to climax with the two lead vocalists harmonizing in the chorus. The lyrics were psychedelic, and dealt with someone who was utterly down and out, trying to get into the light, a theme I used quite a lot later on in my career. The ending vamp featured two vocalists trading riffs back and forth, similar to what the Righteous Brothers did on their record "You've Lost That Lovin' Feelin'"—one of my all-time-favorite songs.

After several days of revamping, I came up with the finished song. I

showed it to the rest of the band and we began rehearsing it in preparation for our trip to London. I was becoming apprehensive about the musical capabilities of the rest of the band, since this song was more rock oriented, a departure from the R&B-oriented show we were used to putting on. I set my concerns aside and reminded myself that Jimmy Miller, our producer, would do his magic in the studio. As we boarded the ferryboat to London, I thought of my distant relative, John Wright—the Lord of Kelvedon Hall in Essex, England—departing with his family in 1640 for America in search of a new life. I was also searching for a new life, ironically in the same country my distant ancestors once inhabited but left to follow their dreams.

Three

SPOOKY TOOTH AND
LONDON IN THE SIXTIES

C hris Blackwell played a pivotal role in my life as a recording artist, placing my career on the map. His own career in music also inspired me to choose music over a degree in clinical psychology. Chris had spent much of his youth in Jamaica, where his family owned large tracts of land. He was sent to England as a young man to attend the prestigious Harrow, a well-known boarding school whose alumni included eight prime ministers, a number of foreign statesmen, as well as two kings. Deciding not to continue his education at a university, he returned to Jamaica and slowly found his way into the local music business there. He started his own record label, Island Records, and enjoyed moderate success with ska music. Returning to England in the early 1960s, he immersed himself in the English music scene and gradually developed a passion for it. Further honing his skills as a record producer, he learned the art of dealing with artists, choosing songs, working with recording engineers, and generally exercising good taste in doing so. In 1964, he produced his first big international hit with Jamaican artist Millie Small's "My Boy Lollipop," which put Island on the map. Chris had a great instinct for knowing what would be success-

ful, having over the years signed artists like Traffic, Cat Stevens, Bob Marley, U2, and Spooky Tooth, to name just a few.

Shortly after arriving in London, The New York Tymes and I met with Chris and Jimmy to discuss a plan for recording our first single, "Sunshine Help Me." Jimmy booked time at Olympic Studios in Barnes—his favorite studio in London—and we rehearsed a little more before going into the studio. Jimmy chose Eddie Kramer to be our engineer. Eddie had just finished working on Jimi Hendrix's and Traffic's first albums, and he went on to work with such legends as The Beatles, The Rolling Stones, Peter Frampton, Joe Cocker, David Bowie, and Led Zeppelin. We were filled with joyous expectation, given our recording team.

The evening of our recording session, however, proved to be a disaster. My earlier apprehensions about the capabilities of the band proved to be embarrassingly correct. What you can get away with musically in live performances doesn't carry over under the microscope of a studio environment. The band was very nervous and played out of time with each other, continually making mistakes. Alone on organ, I wasn't able to keep it all together by myself. After about three hours, we stopped recording and Jimmy tactfully stated that he had enough on tape to work with. I felt otherwise, and after the band left, we both agreed that as musicians they didn't cut it in the studio. I felt terrible about what had transpired, fearing that I might have to go back to playing clubs in Germany. But God had other plans for me.

The next day I met with Chris and discovered all was not lost. He had faith in my songwriting and singing, but not with the rest of the group. I was left with the undesirable task of telling The New York Tymes that I was leaving the band to pursue my own career. I felt bad because we had been through a lot together playing in Germany and the rest of Europe, but inside I knew it was time to move on. Naturally, they were disappointed when we said our goodbyes. With the exception

of Jimmy Carrol, I never saw or heard from any of them again. While I was living in the U.K., I heard Jimmy had released a couple of albums on A&M Records, then we lost contact.

Chris happened to have another band signed to his label called Art—formerly the VIPs—and who had had a big hit in Europe earlier with a track called "I Wanna Be Free." Their singer was Mike Harrison, who had a classic Ray Charles–like husky, bluesy voice. Without really thinking about it, we became a band with two lead vocalists whose voices blended exceptionally well together—kind of like the Righteous Brothers—with me singing the higher parts and Mike the lower ones. We also each played keyboards, though I played the majority of the parts, both live and in the studio. This configuration was something new in the British music scene; everyone in the business reacted very positively to us. The other members of the band were Greg Ridley on bass, Luther Grosvenor on guitar, and Mike Kellie, who we all called "Kellie," on drums. The first rehearsal blew me away. I showed the band my song "Sunshine Help Me" and they quickly learned it. I played organ and sang the lead vocal; Mike and I harmonized the choruses and did the ending vocal ad libs together. It was so much better than The New York Tymes version—I couldn't believe what I was hearing. Luther played a kind of Jimi Hendrix riff in the verses, which really brought the track to life, and Kellie's tumbling drum fills shifted the track in yet another direction, culminating in our bluesy vocal blend. Without planning, it seemed to fit perfectly for the time period we were in.

Near the end of our first rehearsal, Chris arrived and we played him the song. I'll never forget watching his beaming face as we ran through the arrangement. He was very proud that his instinct proved to be successful.

Over the years people have frequently asked me how we came up with the name Spooky Tooth. Chris had called me after our first rehearsal concerned that we desperately needed a name for the band. I

had a friend named Ted Voelkel, who was a close friend of Bill Markle's older brother, Gil. Ted went to Yale, where he met Gil and wrote atonal poetry as a hobby. Ted had an IQ that was off the charts and was very articulate whenever he spoke. We all loved to watch him stand up and recite his atonal poetry fully animated, as if he were reading a news commentary. A sentence might read "Wet Hayshark, a Lugars Groove, Fanny Bourbon and Boastful Snowflakes. Laughing Alps and Satisfied Scallops, Punctual Water-Lillys and Cognition Keys." It was bizarre and hilarious at the same time. He had some pretty wild poems and I decided to call him and explain the dilemma of needing a name for our band. A few days later, I received an envelope with about three pages of possible band names. I arranged a meeting with Chris to go over Ted's list and began reading its contents to him and rest of the group. We spent a lot of time laughing at names like Huffing Shawl, Napa My Valley, and Renegades Agog, but when I came to Spooky Tooth, Chris said, "Yes, I like that," and we all agreed.

The original Spooky Tooth band: Luther Grosvenor, Mike Harrison, Mike Kellie, Gary, Greg Ridley and (possibly) a road manager backstage at a show in England, circa 1968.

We went back into the studio with Jimmy and Eddie to rerecord "Sunshine Help Me." Jimmy wanted to add a special flavor to the track by putting on African drums and it really helped to establish the groove. I played Hammond organ and harpsichord, and Greg, Kellie, Luther, and Mike all gave stellar performances. We recorded it on a four-track tape machine—the standard in the industry at that time—and it all came together wonderfully. I was so thrilled and thankful. Only a few months ago, I was playing clubs in Europe, which was OK at that particular time; but now I was in London—the international and very influential hub of the music business—working with the likes of Jimmy Miller and Chris Blackwell. "Sunshine Help Me" was released as Spooky Tooth's first single and received good air play on British radio and throughout the rest of Europe. It was also hailed in the music press. We were instantly on the map as one of the new and happening bands.

There's an interesting story that's tied to the karma of my song "Sunshine Help Me." Many times during my career I have seen firsthand how the music business is full of surprises when you least expect it. I received an e-mail from someone at Island Records in early 2011 asking permission to use a sample from "Sunshine Help Me" for a track being recorded by Jay Z, Kanye West, Frank Ocean, and The-Dream called "No Church in the Wild." The track was to be included on their upcoming album *Watch the Throne*, which wound up debuting at number 1 on the *Billboard* charts. It was also featured in trailers for the films *Safe House* (2012) and *The Great Gatsby* (2013). And if that wasn't enough, the song won a Grammy for Best Rap/Sung Collaboration at the Fifty-fifth Grammy Awards held in February 2013. All this from the first song I'd ever written professionally nearly forty-seven years earlier. God—the Master Novelist—has always provided for me, consistently dropping wonderful surprises along the path of my life when I least expected it.

After the release of our first single, we began writing songs for our first album. We spent a fair bit of time brainstorming over the general direction and image of the band and how it would stand out from the rest of the groups vying for recognition. This was a concept I'd never heard about in the United States, as most of the focus there was on the songs and singers. But in the U.K., clothes, hairstyles, general look, how interviews were conducted, as well as the spirit of the songs—especially the lyrical content—all were taken into consideration when focusing on the image and direction of a band. These, and of course the talent of the songwriters, musicians, and vocalists, were all factored in. Many times I heard "Yeah, so-and-so band are great musicians but they don't have an image." This line of thinking was exemplified in groundbreaking British bands in the sixties and seventies—the Stones, Beatles, Hendrix, Led Zeppelin, and the Who to name a few—all of which had incredibly magnetic front men. You didn't see that as much in American bands during that time because it didn't seem to be a priority.

So here we were: me, the rest of the band, Chris, and Jimmy trying to conceive a direction for the band. What we had going for us initially was a strong name in Spooky Tooth, two lead vocalists—unusual for the time, good musicianship in the individual members, and the moody vibe the band projected in photos. Songwriting became the challenge, and I was taking advice from both Jimmy and Chris to zero in on the band's direction, both musically and lyrically. My background was soul and R&B, and so was Jimmy's to a certain extent, so we both had to put aside that influence. I was the main songwriter in the band and Jimmy was a good writer as well, so together we wrote several of the songs, which in retrospect weren't the essence of who the band was—a blues/rock psychedelic band with strong lead vocals. Mike's gravelly Ray Charles–like voice, combined with my rock and sometimes high falsetto voice, became our signature. But it wasn't till we got to the next album, *Spooky Two*, that we hit our stride with songs like "Better by

You" and the remake of "Evil Woman," which became progressive rock standards on rock radio.

I was the only American in the band and my relationship with the rest of the members was unique, given that the rest of the group didn't really know Americans and their traits that well. I was pretty good at doing voice impersonations, so the rest of the band was always egging me on to tell them a joke or relate some funny story—usually with a thick Brooklyn or Jersey accent, which they weren't used to but really liked. Then we would trade off, and they would show off some of their regional British accents, which to me were hilarious. We laughed and joked around a lot and slowly became good friends.

Luther had long red hair and projected a strong image—especially apparent when we played live. Growing up in Evesham in the Midlands, he had a band together with Traffic's drummer Jim Capaldi earlier in his career. His playing was technically exceptional, and he would always try to come up with original parts when we were working together on arrangements. I enjoyed writing songs with him, as he would always go the extra mile in trying to make our creation stand out. He was very well respected by other guitarists, and later on in his career went on to play with Mott the Hoople and Stealers Wheel, changing his name to Ariel Bender.

Mike Kellie added a very unique contribution to Spooky Tooth with his unusual style of playing. His feel was loose yet precise, and the drum parts he came up with gave the band a very recognizable sound. Well over six feet tall, with long dark hair down to his shoulders, he was also from the Midlands. We wrote several songs together—lyrics being his specialty. Later on, he played with Peter Frampton's band, Frampton's Camel, as well as with The Only Ones. He also loved getting into long philosophical conversations with me, usually on the long drives to concerts.

Our bass player, Greg Ridley, also projected a very cool image on-

stage and had impeccable taste in what he wore both on and offstage. A lot of his wardrobe consisted of custom-made jackets, trousers, shirts, and boots, and he knew the best shops and tailors in London. Tall and very slim, he added a strong visual element to the band. Greg set the wardrobe example for the rest of us to follow. His bass playing was simple but very powerful, and he also sang strong backing vocals. After Spooky Tooth, he became one of the founding members of Humble Pie.

Mike Harrison and I had a close and friendly relationship. We even shared a mews cottage in Belgravia, London, for a period of time. Mike had a great voice—probably one of the best blues/rock voices that came out of the U.K. at that time. Quite thin, with long, dark brown curly hair down to his shoulders, he had a voice that contributed a lot to the band's sound. I sang the higher parts—sometimes in a falsetto voice— and he sang the lower; this combination became the band's trademark. Mike was great at imitating a Scottish accent—especially the Glasgow version—and we spent hours belly-laughing together. The band all lived in London, and Chris bought us a Ford sedan so we could drive back and forth to our shows. Mike drove and I was the navigator using a AAA road atlas. After some time I became quite good at finding venues in very out-of-the-way places. I also fell in love with the English countryside.

One of the elements that made Spooky Tooth stand out was our cover versions of well-known songs, radically rearranged. The blues classic "Tobacco Road" and Janis Ian's "Society's Child" were covers that appeared on our first album, both slowed down considerably and rearranged. Fitting into my new role as a songwriter was initially daunting. I had always liked my English classes in both high school and college—I had minored in English—but writing lyrics that were both unusual and rhyming was a challenge. That, and learning how to co-write songs with the other members of the band or with Jimmy, was un-

explored territory for me, but I accepted it as a growth experience. For our first album, *It's All About*, I wrote one song alone—our earlier single "Sunshine Help Me"—and cowrote the rest of the material, with either Jimmy or other members of the band. The recording sessions went very well and I absorbed a lot watching Jimmy and Eddie work together. My favorite tracks were "Tobacco Road" and "Society's Child." They captured the essence of the band, with its dual lead vocals over radically slowed-down, driving, bluesy tracks. I wasn't yet satisfied with my songwriting abilities in general and felt I needed to write songs on our next albums that would incorporate more of the strengths of the band. I felt I needed to hone in more on the band's musical direction.

It's All About had moderate success in both the U.K. and the United States, and did quite well in Europe—especially Germany. We spent most of 1968 touring the U.K. or abroad, and writing songs on days off. During this period, we also made our first tour of the States, which was fun for me—returning home as a member of a British rock band. Most people assumed I was British as well because I had picked up an accent while living there and because we were always billed as a rock band from Great Britain. To this day, many people still think I'm English. Once, a Scotsman in a discussion with my wife, Rose, even insisted I was a Brit. On tour, however, I went along with this assumption and had a lot of fun with it.

Many Americans weren't at all used to dealing with British rock bands; instead, their frame of reference was the singing groups that dominated U.S. charts. We were in New York City staying at the Loews hotel in Manhattan at one point, and ordered breakfast in the hotel's coffee shop. Our waitress had a huge bouffant hairdo and wore thick makeup. When we started ordering, she exclaimed, "Hey, geez—watta yooz guys, in a singin' group? I love your accents, keep tawkin'." We all burst out laughing. On another occasion, our car was towed after our road manager, Danny Farnham, had double-parked in a tow-away zone

on Eighth Avenue. He went to the bellman and said, "Look here, I've got a hired car that's been impounded." The bellman immediately answered, "What's dat buddy, ya gotta hot car?" Accents are always fun to play with.

The first show of our first American tour was at Bill Graham's Fillmore West in August 1968. On the bill was Cold Blood and Quicksilver Messenger Service. We had literally just arrived in San Francisco from London and were driven straight to the show, walking onstage to perform with no sound check. Miraculously, we pulled it off and the audience was very receptive to our music. Bill Graham invited us to come back and play again, and became our friend and champion.

The late sixties were still early days for rock bands touring the States. A lot of bugs still needed to be worked out with stage equipment, instrument rentals, PA systems, and even choosing concert agents. It was also a time of change culturally, and people were only slowly starting to get used to men wearing long hair. Several shows into the tour, we were somehow booked to play at a college dance—definitely *not* the right venue for our kind of music. Most of the men attending wore Madras jackets and had crew cuts. They must have thought we would be playing middle-of-the-road dance music—certainly not progressive rock. After we'd played a few songs, a fraternity guy came up to the stage and said, "Aah, come on, fellas—can't you play a nice waltz or somethin'?" In response, Kellie stood up and pushed his drum kit off the riser onto the floor. Blown away by the surreal encounter, we all ran offstage together and, jumping into our van, we sped off.

On another occasion during our first U.S. tour, Spooky Tooth were asked to perform during the seventh inning stretch at a baseball game at Dodger Stadium in Los Angeles. We set up all our equipment on a moveable stage and were towed onto the field by a tractor. As we got closer to the infield, the fans started booing and screaming, "Hey, get your hair cut." I felt like a Christian at the Roman Coliseum being

thrown to the lions. At the end of our performance, a lot of people cheered—but their cheering was not quite loud enough to overcome the booing!

Chris had big ambitions for our next album and decided to give us use of a farm he owned in Theale, Berkshire, about an hour west of London in the English countryside. The farm was on a lake and was a source of continual inspiration. We converted one of the rooms into our rehearsal hall, where we would practice and write. We had a housekeeper who looked like someone out of a horror movie. We eventually had to dismiss her. I spent many hours outside near the lake or in my bedroom writing on my acoustic guitar. Lyrically, I was writing stories about people tossed on the waves of their emotions, going off to fight in wars or overcoming personal internal conflicts; that seemed to enhance Mike's and my style of singing. My guitar playing was getting better; I was coming up with blues riffs that I knew Luther and Greg would enhance, adding their own style to what I had written and making the end result even better. It was a wonderful time in my life creatively and I felt fulfilled with my progress as a writer, singer, and player.

Toward the end of 1968, we went into the studio to record our next and, in my opinion, best album. To play off our name, we called it *Spooky Two*. Island's fold of artists had increased, and we were touring and hanging out with several artists who were either managed or signed to the label, including Traffic, Joe Cocker, and Free. We were like a big family working in a very loose and friendly atmosphere, both in touring and in the studio. During the recording of *Spooky Two*, Steve Winwood played piano on "I've Got Enough Heartaches," Joe Cocker sang backing vocals on "Feelin' Bad," Dave Mason played guitar on "That Was Only Yesterday," and Jimmy played drums on "Hangman Hang My Shell on a Tree." Andy Johns, who was our assistant engineer on *It's All About*, engineered the album, and once again we used Olympic Studios.

Mike Kellie and Gary at the lake next to Spooky Tooth's farm in Theale, Berkshire, England.

Jimmy and Andy made a great team in the studio figuring out ways to enhance our tracks with repeat echoes or delays and other toys, working in the control room while we were in the studio fine-tuning our arrangements. After doing a take and listening to what we had recorded, we were always surprised with what Jimmy and Andy had added sonically to the tracks.

Working with Jimmy on our first two albums was incredible. He was a producer's producer, in that he was not only a musician but a writer as well and could restructure songs to make them stronger in a matter of moments. Over six feet tall, outgoing and gregarious, Jimmy was larger than life. In the studio, he was magnetic regardless of the level of fame of the artists he was dealing with. When listening to playbacks, he would close his eyes and rock back and forth absorbing the music. At times when doing so, he would suddenly jump up and start singing a part he heard in his head that would usually greatly enhance the arrangement. If you posed a question, he would look you straight in the eye while twirling his mustache, deeply thinking. After a minute

or so, he'd give you his take on the matter. Jimmy also had a great sense of humor—especially when receiving the check in restaurants. He would pretend to scrutinize the bill holding it close to his face and then jump up and shout at the waiter, "For what?" He also wrote some great lyrics in his career, such as "I'm a Man," which was the second hit single by The Spencer Davis Group, after "Gimme Some Lovin'," and also a huge hit by Chicago a few years later. His engineering instincts in the studio were riveting and even inspirational. Later on in his career, when he was producing the Stones, he told me that when the feel for "Honky Tonk Women" wasn't happening, he picked up a cowbell, ran into the studio, and started playing along with the band. The track suddenly came together a few minutes later. He became my mentor along my path of becoming a producer later on.

Spooky Two went Top 40 on the U.S. *Billboard* album charts and did very well in Europe as well—especially in Germany, where we were voted one of the top five bands in 1969. In my opinion, it was the best album we made because the band was playing really well together and our musical direction was focused. I had also come into my own as a songwriter, arranger, and co-vocalist. And, of course, Jimmy's production ideas were a constant source of inspiration for us. Probably most important, there were no personality problems hampering the creative flow of our music.

I wound up writing four of the eight songs on the album and co-wrote the rest with Luther, Kellie, and Mike, with the exception of "Evil Woman," which was written by Larry Weiss and recorded by Lou Rawls. Requests for TV appearances and world tours started flowing in, and we got tighter as a band, playing shows and festivals with other artists such as Jimi Hendrix, The Rolling Stones, Ten Years After, Janis Joplin, Cat Stevens, Traffic, and Jethro Tull. Radio picked up on the band as well. In the United States and U.K., stations began playing "Tobacco Road" from the first album and "Evil Woman" and "Better

by You, Better than Me" from *Spooky Two*. In Germany and the rest of Europe, my song "That Was Only Yesterday" became a big hit on mainstream radio. I was thrilled at the success we were enjoying.

At my first music publisher Lionel Conway's sixtieth birthday bash recently, Chris Blackwell reminded me of a story regarding Jethro Tull. One afternoon I was in Chris's office, having some business there, and he asked me out of the blue, "I'm looking for a blues band to add to my artist rostrum. Do you have any ideas?" I thought for a moment and answered, "As a matter of fact I do. We played last week at a university in Lincoln and the opening act was really good. Their music had a bluesy/jazz flavor to it and was very original sounding. I was quite impressed by them. The lead singer played flute really well and created a persona onstage the likes of which I've not seen before." Chris smiled and thanked me. The next thing I knew, Jethro Tull got signed to Island Records through a deal with Chrysalis Records.

Lionel Conway joined Island's publishing company in 1969. He came from Dick James Music, and I had recommended him to Chris because I felt he had good taste in the writers he had previously signed. He was managing Elton John at the time, who was then an up-and-coming songwriter, and Lionel was influential in getting Elton signed to the Dick James label. During that time, Spooky Tooth covered one of Elton's songs, "Son of Your Father," which was released as a single in 1969. Lionel gave me a lot of encouragement in my songwriting and was a real friend—someone I could turn to when I needed serious advice about my career. Later on, he was also instrumental in finding and signing Robert Palmer, Cat Stevens, and U2 to Island.

In late 1969, a French affiliate of the Dutch company Phillips Records contacted Island, asking them if Spooky Tooth would be interested in collaborating with Pierre Henry, a French electronic music composer. Electronic music at that time, predating Moog modular synthesizers, consisted of using different kinds of tone generators such

as the Theremin to create weird avant-garde sounds. Beginning in the 1940s, Henry and his collaborator, Pierre Schaeffer, experimented with recording natural sounds, the human voice, mechanical sounds—stretching and contorting them, creating what Henry called "electro-acoustic" music. Chris broached the concept to us, but having just come off the success of *Spooky Two*, we weren't interested in making such a radical left turn in our career. After some convincing on his part, we agreed, so long as it was released as a Pierre Henry album and not the follow-up to *Spooky Two*. I would write the music to an electronic Catholic Mass titled *Ceremony*, and the band would perform and record it—like session musicians.

We recorded it in about a week's time and Pierre then took our master and overdubbed his electronic music to our two-track recording—not to the four-track master, which would have been the correct way of doing it. The balance between our music and his music really bothered us because at times the electronic music was much louder than our voices and tracks. When it came time to release *Ceremony*, Chris dropped the bomb on us saying it was going to be the new Spooky Tooth album and that it was going to do very well. We all were shocked and couldn't believe the turn of events. I personally felt betrayed, tricked, and angry that he would do this against our better judgment, especially after the success of our last album. Moreover, if we had released another album as good as or better than *Spooky Two*, we could have had a huge career.

That singular decision took the wind out of our sails, careerwise. But as he was our manager and owner of the record company, we had to honor his decision. In 1970, the album was released and it tanked, as we thought it would. Group morale was at an all-time low. Drug and personality problems began to develop within the band; Greg left to join Humble Pie and I decided to leave and pursue a solo career—a desire

that had been silently growing within me since we started recording *Ceremony*. The idea of being a solo artist was very exciting to me, especially the prospect of not having to divide into five parts the decision-making process about what to do or not do—the dilemma every band goes through. In retrospect, I think I would have gone solo at some point regardless of what happened with *Ceremony*. Spooky Tooth released another album after I left called *The Last Puff*, using members from Joe Cocker's Grease Band along with Mike, Luther, and Kellie. On a positive note, the album had a great version of John Lennon's "I Am the Walrus," which Mike sang incredibly well.

Shortly after leaving the band, I got an offer from Jimmy Miller to work for his new production company, Ringmaker Music. Jimmy invited me to temporarily live with him and his girlfriend, Gerry, at their flat on Cromwell Road in West London until I got my feet on the ground financially. I had previously been subsidized by Island; now Jimmy would be my benefactor. Jim Capaldi and Dave Mason had the flat opposite Jimmy's, which I took over when they moved out. I started working for Ringmaker, producing various artists like Steve Gibbons and Sky—who became The Knack later on. Andy Johns was still working with me as an engineer, and later on I began working with Chris Kimsey as well. Jimmy had been my mentor as a producer, but now I was learning a lot of tricks in the studio from Andy and Chris. They went on to have stellar careers as both engineers and producers, working with such artists as the Rolling Stones, Led Zeppelin, Humble Pie, and Peter Frampton.

Jimmy got an offer from Mick Jagger to produce the Rolling Stones. It was a huge boost in his career and he was beside himself. He invited me down to one of the sessions at Olympic where they were recording "Jumpin' Jack Flash." I was in awe witnessing musical history—the band sounded great. Jimmy would bring home rough mixes of tracks he

had just recorded—"Honky Tonk Women," "Sympathy for the Devil," and "Street Fighting Man," to name a few. I was impressed with the great work he was doing.

Over the course of his work with the Stones, I went to several of the sessions and became friendly with Charlie Watts, the Stones' drummer, who was a wonderful human being. I never felt intimidated around him and he was always so easy to talk with. Charlie and I used to hang out at a small restaurant right next to the studio, and we'd have a coffee or a bowl of soup and talk about our common passion—music. He loved jazz and so did I. We chatted about the wonderful concerts I attended in New York in the Village in the early sixties, seeing artists like guitarist Wes Montgomery and the iconic Dave Brubeck. I met Wes Montgomery at a club in lower Manhattan one night and asked him why he played using his thumb rather than a pick. He told me that when he practiced at home, his neighbor living below him would bang on the wall. In desperation, Wes threw the pick down and started playing with his thumb, which wasn't nearly as loud. At his next concert he started playing with a pick again but felt totally inhibited and, throwing it on the floor, never used one again—only his thumb, which became his trademark. Charlie shook his head and laughed at the story.

In between production projects, I began writing songs for what would be my first solo album. Jimmy offered to finance and release the album through his production company. I wanted it to be a rock album, since that was my frame of reference from having been in Spooky Tooth. Ironically, the songs I wrote for my first solo effort would have been the follow-up to *Spooky Two*. After considering all my options, I began putting together a group of musicians I had known or played with before, including Alan White (Yes); Trevor Burton (The Move); Klaus Voormann (Plastic Ono Band); Mick Abrahams (Jethro Tull); Mike Kellie; and my old friend from New Jersey, Hugh McCracken (Wings, John Lennon, and Steely Dan). I had always admired Hugh's

playing, from the time he appeared with his group The Shakes at clubs in New Jersey. When I felt comfortable with the songs I had written specifically for the album—all on my nylon-string acoustic guitar—I called Olympic and booked the time for recording and mixing the album. Andy Johns was once again my engineer. I was so thankful to have been given this opportunity to make my own album and Andy did a brilliant job engineering it. God was once again lighting the path for me—even though the ride proved to be bumpy along the way. Jimmy chose the name *Extraction* for the album—a pun on my having left

This drawing by Klaus Voormann was featured on the *Extraction* album cover.

Spooky Tooth; Klaus Voormann did the album cover—unique but in the same style as the Beatles' *Revolver* cover, which he had recently done. I was thrilled with the results of my first solo effort.

Spooky Two and *Ceremony* had been released on A&M Records in the United States, and I already had a good working relationship with them—especially Chuck Kaye, who was then in charge of their artists and repertoire (A&R) department. When *Extraction* was finished, I send a copy to Chuck to get his feedback. A few days later, he called me raving how he wanted the album for A&M. I was thrown into a conflict immediately, given that Jimmy had financed the project and was meant to be releasing it through his production company with his partner Tony Secunda. Intuitively, I was not very secure with Jimmy and Tony's strengths outside of the studio in the music business world. Would my album realize its full potential being released through their company?

To make matters even more tense, the A&M team, including the company's co-founder and CEO, Jerry Moss; its president, Gil Friesen; their legal counsel, Abe Somer; and of course Chuck Kaye, all arrived in London a week or so later to discuss business with me. We met at my flat to listen to my album and discuss a proposal they had put together. Jerry Moss offered a deal that I could hardly refuse, part of which involved buying out Jimmy and Tony, and releasing *Extraction* on their label. I was thrown into a loyalty conflict. On one side was my long friendship with Jimmy, and on the other was an offer from a successful record label that was totally excited and seemingly very committed to my album. Betrayal is perhaps one of the hardest emotions to deal with, and on one level I felt I was betraying Jimmy and throwing aside all he had done for me. But this was my career, and I couldn't throw that away. I had to do what would give my album its best possible chance. I called Jimmy and told him I wanted to go with A&M. He was very upset at my decision and our relationship never fully recovered, although it did improve with time.

Extraction was released in 1971 and became a radio hit in the United States, and critically acclaimed in the media, but it never succeeded

commercially. That, compounded with my loss of Jimmy as a friend, devastated me. I still felt I had made the right decision in going with A&M, and I wasn't ready yet to quit. But I had been on an emotional roller coaster already with Spooky Tooth, having released three albums of which only one was moderately successful.

Success, I was learning, is something you create over several lifetimes. It doesn't just fall into your lap. You attract conditions, opportunities, partners, and all the elements you need in direct proportion to the good karma you have created in the past. And when the seeds of that karma are ready to germinate, when the conditions are favorable, life rearranges itself and you begin to harvest the bounty of your continuous efforts from the past. There are no givens; it takes sustained hard work. I always remind myself of the adage "A successful man is someone who fails 90 percent of the time but picks himself up after each attempt—never giving up."

Shortly before leaving Spooky Tooth, I met Christina, who was from Sweden, during a short vacation I was having in Los Angeles. My sister Beverly introduced us. She was very beautiful and I immediately became infatuated with her. At this point in my life, I was really ready to get into a serious relationship with someone. We fell in love, and she came back to England with me. We rented a lovely apartment in Chelsea, a short walk from the Thames River. We both loved good food and she was a great cook. I was twenty-six and she was twenty-three when we decided to get married. Over the next few years, we had two boys, Justin born in 1971, and Dorian born in 1973. We moved out of London shortly after Dorian was born and bought a four-story Georgian town house at 2 Trinity Place, Windsor, Berkshire, where we stayed until we moved back to the United States.

Emotionally, I welcomed the big adjustment of having one, and then two, babies in my life. I've always loved children. With this first time being a father, I experienced a paternal love, one I'd never felt before. It

With wife Christina and son Justin, 1976.
(© Bruce Kessler.)

was a very touching time for me, especially telling stories to the boys before they fell asleep at night or going to the zoo or on other outings in London. These are moments I will always treasure and the good news is that I get to do this all again—not the career part, but the baby part—with my two granddaughters.

Had God not put that love in our hearts, we wouldn't be able to love our children and family as we do. It is through loving our family members and close friends that we slowly expand that love until it encompasses all humanity. Love is a huge force in creation and is constantly drawing and attracting everything back to God.

This was also a period of reflection for me. So far, my life had had a lot of ups and downs, but I was able to handle them because I had a

deep faith in myself and God—knowing that somehow everything would be all right. But there was still an undercurrent running through my life that manifested as a fear of death. I knew it came from my near-death experience when I was sixteen, but I didn't yet have the tools or wisdom to resolve it. "Why am I here and what is the goal of life?" I would often ask myself, but never came up with a satisfactory answer. Trying to talk with other people about such things was like the blind leading the blind, and they would usually change the subject if I broached it in conversation. I began to realize that most human beings never take the time to question the meaning of their existence or why they are here. It's too scary. It wasn't until later on, when I became firmly established on my spiritual path, that I realized that life's purpose was to find God by uniting your soul with His Consciousness. Once you begin to do that, you see that life becomes simpler and has a beautiful purpose.

My guru once said, "The greatest love you can experience is in communion with God in meditation. The love between soul and Spirit is the perfect love, the love you are all seeking. When you meditate, love grows. Millions of thrills pass through your heart. . . . If you strive to love all and to meditate more deeply, there will come into your life such love as you never dreamed possible."[6]

Four

I MEET GEORGE

"To Discover Yourself"

WRITTEN BY GEORGE HARRISON
AND GARY WRIGHT

Out of all the lies that I can recall
Breaking and destroying worlds appears to be the favorite of them all
All these childish games left me hanging low
Forcing me into myself I found a place from where I felt my love grow
To discover your Self you'll deliver yourself from darkness and soon
 you'll see
To discover your Self you'll recover the wealth of everything that you
 could be
Let yourself unwind soon enough you'll find
Sadness disappearing in a light that shines with truth and lights up
 your mind
To discover your Self you'll deliver your Self from darkness and soon
 you'll see
To discover your Self you'll recover the wealth of everything that you
 could be—you'll be free

went back to producing various artists, writing songs, and playing sessions in London—slowly returning back to normal after *Extraction* had fizzled. Chuck and Gil from A&M Records would call me regularly to get an update on my next project with their label. They were still very interested in my career as a solo artist. Producers began calling me, asking if I would be interested in playing on various projects. On one such occasion I got a call from Richard Perry, who was in London producing Harry Nilsson's new album, and he asked me if I was interested in playing piano on a few tracks. I was very pleased at the invitation as I was a big fan of Harry's voice as well as his songwriting. I played piano on "Without You" and organ on "Let the Good Times Roll." When released, the album was titled *Nilsson Schmilsson*, and "Without You" became a huge hit worldwide. I was very touched by being given the opportunity to contribute my piano part to such a great song and outstanding vocal by Harry.

During that period we had a flat on Curzon Place, a very sought-after area in London. But I needed a larger place as my family was running out of space and Harry offered to buy it from me. He had the flat redecorated, using a design firm co-owned by Ringo Starr. Curzon Place was opposite the Playboy Club, and the flat became a crash pad for many of Harry's friends. Sadly, first Mama Cass and then Keith Moon died there, in the same bedroom. There were many family memories associated with the flat, and although I never met either of them, both their deaths were very disturbing to me.

During that period, I also played piano and organ on the *B.B. King in London* album, which included performances by Ringo, Steve Winwood, Dr. John, and Steve Marriott. I also wrote one of the songs on the album, "Wet Hayshark," an instrumental that we put together in the studio. B.B. was a very gentle, sweet soul and had some great sto-

ries to relate about growing up in the South as a young musician. His unique style of playing carved a path for many great blues guitarists who arrived later on the music scene. When we were recording, he gave me complete latitude to play what I felt was right for the track we were working on. After one session when Ringo was playing drums and I was on organ, we were in the control room listening to the track we had just recorded. B.B. looked at Ringo and said, "Man, you keep time like a big clock." I smiled at Ringo and remembered an old saying I'd once heard: "Humility is a sign of greatness." It certainly was manifest in B.B.

I had admired Jerry Lee Lewis from when I first started playing piano at age fourteen. The very first song I learned to play by ear was "Whole Lotta Shakin' Goin' On." In one period, when I was playing on a lot of sessions, I got a call that Jerry Lee was looking for musicians to play on his new album. I was invited to come to the studio, where the usual group of musicians had gathered, including Alvin Lee, Ringo, Klaus Voormann, myself, and Eric Clapton. Initially, Eric appeared to be shy and reclusive, but over time he opened up. I played with him on *All Things Must Pass* and several other George Harrison albums, and he became one of my favorite guitar players. I don't think I ever heard him make a mistake when he played; he always came up with great parts when in the studio and was an inspiration to work with. To my way of thinking, his performance with Cream on "Sunshine of Your Love" is one of the best rock tracks ever recorded. Jerry Lee asked me to play organ on several tracks during the course of the evening. His piano playing was still great, and that night fulfilled a dream I'd secretly harbored over the years: to meet and play with "The Killer" himself . . . Jerry Lee Lewis.

London was definitely the hot place to be in the early seventies, and many American musicians were coming over to be a part of that scene. I would play fairly regularly with Jim Keltner or Jim Gordon

(drums), Jerry Donahue (guitar), Bobby Whitlock (keyboards), Jim Price (trumpet or trombone), and Bobby Keys (sax)—all transplants from the States.

I met Mick Jones during that period. He called me and invited me to play on Johnny Hallyday's new album, which was being recorded at Olympic Studios. Mick and Tommy Brown were Johnny's musical directors, and they wrote most of his songs at that time. Johnny was a huge star in French-speaking countries worldwide. Known as "the Elvis of France," to his fans, he was a larger-than-life, reckless James Dean kind of character, sporting motorcycle jackets and tight jeans and always looking cool—especially when he was riding his bike. But behind all that was a very artistic, real person whose career has endured over decades.

Johnny liked recording in London and always invited top musicians to play on his records—Peter Frampton and Jimmy Page, to name a few. I had a good feeling about working with Mick, and after a few sessions he invited me to write or contribute songs for the new album they were working on. One of the songs I wrote that Johnny recorded was called "Wildfire," from a Spooky Tooth album. In French, the title was "Le Feu." It became a big hit for Johnny, and he still performs it in his live shows to this day. Johnny looked and played the part well of being a French rock star, at times arriving at shows or clubs with a group of friends, all on motorcycles. He very kindly invited me to be his opening act at the Palais des Sports—Paris's largest performance venue to perform in in the early seventies. My band consisted of Mick (who wasn't playing in Johnny's band at the time) on guitar, Bryson Graham on drums, Archie Legget on bass, and me on vocals and keyboards. We performed there for about two weeks, and after the shows, would hang out at Johnny's huge, beautifully decorated modern apartment in a very cool part of Paris. Every now and then during those evenings, I would borrow one of his acoustic guitars and play him a song I was working

on. He would always listen carefully and then give me his input as to whether he thought the song would work for him. We developed a good relationship over time, which continues to this day.

It was at this time that I lived in France for about two months, staying with a friend, Patrick Legrand, brother of the composer Michel. Patrick worked for the French affiliate of the publishing company I was signed to in the United States, Almo/Irving Music, which was owned by Jerry Moss and Herb Alpert, a part of A&M Records. Those were the days when record companies and publishing companies wined and dined their artists and arranged writing sessions with their local writers. The French have always respected artists and musicians, something I personally experienced when I lived there, and I fell in love with Paris. Each moment in the city seemed to draw out a new inspiration in me: around every corner was a beautiful sculpture, park, imaginative storefront, or view of the Seine River.

Mick also had a home in a little country village just outside of Rouen, in Normandy. The house had a thatched roof, stucco walls, and exposed beams on the outside. Stucco ceilings interspersed with wooden beams and rustic plank floors added to the charm inside. I was intrigued by the huge fireplace in the living room—it was big enough to walk in and out of. Firewood in about four-foot lengths was neatly stacked outside. I knew about building a fire from camping in my youth, but I couldn't imagine anyone starting a fire with wood that size. When we first arrived at the house, it was autumn and a bit chilly, and the caretaker offered to light a fire for us. I was very curious about how he would accomplish this, as there was no gas starter or even kindling. First he rolled newspaper into balls and placed them on the bottom of the hearth. Then came the four-foot logs placed on the iron grate, and finally about six or eight long candles on top of the wood. He lit the paper, which started melting the wax, which set both the logs and wax on fire in a matter of minutes. I was impressed with his technique.

The house was right on the fairway of a golf course, and the scenery outside was very pastoral—especially with the beautiful fall colors. My sister Lorna flew over from Los Angeles to spend some time with me, and she made some amazing meals for us. She loved shopping in the little village for fresh baguettes, cheese, and local produce, trying out her fairly good French on the locals. Mick and I did a lot of writing together during that time, and he turned me on to some amazing restaurants in the area.

After my sojourn in France, I returned home to London, and as I was going through my mail, I received a phone call from one of the secretaries at A&M Records. "Hi, Gary," her cheerful voice rang out. "There's a Willy Bogner from Germany who's been trying to reach you. Apparently he's a big fan of Spooky Tooth and he's directing a new movie named *Benjamin*. He wants to talk to you about composing the score for the film." I was both fascinated and flattered at the invitation. I called him back and we spoke for quite some time about the project he was working on. He was friendly and his flawless English was quite impressive. At the end of the conversation we agreed to meet in London to discuss the project. I did some research on him and discovered that not only was he a major cinematographer—having shot the complicated ski chase sequences in earlier James Bond movies—but that he and his family also owned the Bogner line of clothing, specializing in very high-end skiwear. He could also film while skiing backward! When he was eighteen, he competed at the 1960 Winter Olympics for West Germany in Squaw Valley. After leading the competition in the men's slalom in the first run, however, he unfortunately fell during his second run.

Our first meeting took place at my flat in Mayfair, and as we shook hands and greeted each other, I intuitively felt that Willy was someone I was destined to meet. God has always dropped diamonds of experiences along the pathway of my life and this was one of them. I had

never scored a film in my life, but the prospect of doing so was very appealing to me—even though I worried over my inexperience. He was warm and open as he laid out his concept of the music for *Benjamin*, which had already been filmed. It turned out that the protagonist, Benjamin, drifted in and out of dreamlike fantasy flights when he heard certain kinds of music or encountered certain people in his life that triggered these fantasies. This was right up my alley: I was always a big fan of surrealism whether in films or art. I quickly realized how important the score would be for this kind of movie and wanted very much to see what he had already filmed. At the end of our meeting, Willy told me he had arranged a screening room to view the film the next day.

I arrived filled with anticipation. As the playback rolled, I couldn't believe what I was seeing. The cinematography was absolutely breathtaking. The story line was simple but effective, largely consisting of Benjamin's fantasy sojourns while skiing through the Alps and Canadian Rockies, alone or with his dream lover. Music was already flowing through my mind as I watched one spectacular scene after another unfold. When the last reel of film finished, I congratulated Willy on his work and told him I would love to be involved in his project. We met a few more times to discuss technical details as well as the kinds of musical textures he envisioned throughout the movie—scene by scene. As we said our goodbyes, I knew I had met someone whose creative vision was very similar to mine—my visual counterpart.

I spent the next month writing music for the different scenes Willy had mapped out for me. Once again, I did this on my acoustic guitar, writing riffs along with romantic songs for the love scenes. I assembled the same group of musicians I had used in France when I played with Johnny—Mick on guitar, Bryson on drums, Archie on bass, and me on piano and organ. Willy flew back to London for the recording sessions. All went very well. Mick was really helpful in coming up with great parts throughout the sessions. In retrospect, it's amazing for me

to think that I was able to accomplish all this without the use of synthesizers—they just weren't readily available at that time. When we finished recording and mixing the music cues, we all went into the control room at Olympic Studios and played back the music while running the film. I was overjoyed when I saw the marriage of the music I'd composed with Willy's stunning footage—my first soundtrack and the beginning of a new friendship that would last for decades. During the 1980s and '90s, I wound up doing music for two of his other films—*Fire and Ice*, which won the German equivalent of an Oscar, and *Ski to the Max*. The soundtrack for *Fire and Ice* also produced a Top 10 single and album.

There are times we go through in our lives when our careers are running along wonderfully, our personal relationships are great, our health is fine, but something is still missing that we can't pinpoint; something of a spiritual nature that demands our deepest attention. I was at that place in my life, trying to solve my dilemma one afternoon when the phone rang. "Gary. It's Mick here. I have a friend who teaches Transcendental Meditation if you're at all interested in checking it out. I can arrange a meeting with him if you like." I had just walked into my flat and was immediately interested in Mick's news.

"My friend's name is Ron Altbach and he's a teacher and disciple of Maharishi Mahesh Yogi, whom the Beatles visited in India in the mid-1960s. You're given a mantra and they teach you the basics of meditation."

Even as a boy, I had been fascinated by the power of the human mind and had even become interested in hypnotism for a short while. I visited a hypnotherapist to cure myself of a stubborn nail-biting habit and it worked. During my first session, the therapist remarked that he rarely met patients who were able to reach such deep states of relaxation. I never practiced; it came naturally to me, making it easier for him to plant the seed in my subconscious mind to rid myself of the

habit. So this offer of learning to meditate was very appealing. Mick put me in contact with Ron and Ron gave me my first mantra. TM taught me how to concentrate by focusing on a mantra, which then brought peace and relaxation. At that particular time in my spiritual evolution, this was what I needed to do. I continued practicing daily until I found my guru's teachings and spiritual path in 1976. During the late seventies, Ron and I met again when I was on tour and doing several shows opening for the Beach Boys. He was their keyboard player and was very accomplished. God's drama never ceases to amaze me when you look at the big picture, watching different characters come in and out of your life like scenes in a movie—sometimes under the strangest of circumstances. But the more aware you become, the more you see the cosmic script unfold as it does—even sometimes intuiting the subtle reasons and lessons behind these encounters.

I began to concentrate my time again on songwriting, playing on sessions, and producing artists. The English music business at that time was indeed very cool. Often I would spend Sunday afternoons at the home of my friend music publisher Lionel Conway, and from time to time Elton John (then Reg Dwight) would drop by. Elton was doing a lot of songwriting at the time and was trying to get covers on his songs. During those casual afternoons, we would each play new songs that we were working on, getting Lionel's feedback. After Elton got signed to a record deal at DJM, he recorded the album under the title *Elton John*. He called, asking if I would like to hear the album, which he was understandably very proud of, so I invited him to my flat for a small listening party. His songwriting, piano playing, and vocals throughout the album were impressive, especially the track "The Border Song," and I was happy at the huge degree of success he achieved after it was released. We saw each other from time to time over the next few years.

I had learned a lot about making records from Jimmy Miller, and I spent a fair amount of time working at Olympic Studios in Barnes pro-

ducing various artists, usually with Chris Kimsey or Andy Johns as engineers. One afternoon in the spring of 1970, the phone rang in the control room where I was recording.

"There's a call from a Klaus Voormann for you, Gary. Shall I put him through?"

"Sure, put him through," I answered. I hadn't spoken with Klaus in quite some time and was curious as to why he was calling. The last time we spoke was nearly a year earlier, when he had played on *Extraction*. At that moment, I had no idea that what I was about to hear would soon alter the direction of my life.

"Klaus, how are you? It's been a while."

Before I could say anything else, he quickly replied, "Gary, I'm in the studio with George Harrison. Phil Spector is producing George's new album and wants an additional keyboard player for the song they're working on. Can you come to Abbey Road Studios now, as George is keen to get started?" The import of those words resonated through my entire being. I was a huge Beatles fan and especially loved George's amazing track "Within You Without You" from *Sgt. Pepper's*, with its East Indian flavors.

"Wow, are you serious? Of course, I'll be there in just a little bit," I finally answered. I was so elated that I felt like morphing into a James Brown double-split and then breaking into "I Feel Good!" I didn't only because I felt my engineer Chris Kimsey might think I had flipped out.

I left Olympic Studios in a daze and arrived at Abbey Road Studios about a half hour later. I had heard a lot about the studio and its history with George Martin and the Beatles over the years, but being there at that moment was quite overwhelming. I walked into the studio where the recording session was taking place—the same studio where the Beatles had recorded most of their music—and Klaus warmly greeted me. I immediately spotted George Harrison at the other side of the studio; we made eye contact, and he smiled and walked over to greet

me. He was dressed in traditional Indian white pajamas and brown sandals. His long, straight, dark brown hair was parted in the middle and reached halfway down his back; he had a fairly long beard and mustache that covered a good part of his face. I could smell the patchouli oil he was wearing as well as the incense that was burning in the studio.

His brown eyes were penetrating yet peaceful, and he immediately disarmed my nervousness with his gentleness. Meeting someone of his stature was challenging for me at first. I had really never met anyone quite like George before; he didn't seem to be on some huge ego trip like other artists I had met over the years. His aura was calm, and his being exuded a subtle spiritual magnetism. Yet, at the same time, he was someone who was very focused in the here and now. As he shook my hand and graciously introduced himself to me, all the initial apprehensiveness I had been feeling suddenly vanished. I felt in my heart that I was meeting an old friend that I hadn't seen in years—or maybe lifetimes.

He introduced me to the other musicians playing on the track, including Ringo, Eric Clapton, Billy Preston, Klaus Voormann, Jim Gordon, and Badfinger. The group had been rehearsing the song "Isn't It a Pity" when I arrived. George took his acoustic guitar and began showing me the chord changes, which I nervously wrote out on a chord chart. I was making a fair amount of mistakes trying to learn the arrangement while playing along with the band. After a little while, the red "record" light in the studio came on and I still wasn't quite sure of the structure of the song. Then the worst that could happen happened. Producer Phil Spector's voice rang out from the control room into the studio where all the musicians were: "Wait a minute, wait a minute; who's that on the Wurlitzer piano making all those mistakes?" Devastated and utterly embarrassed, I meekly raised my hand and said, "Sorry

it's me, Gary, and I'm still learning the structure of the song." George immediately walked over to me and said consolingly, "Take all the time you need, we're in no rush." He was so kind at that moment; I immediately felt a rapport with him.

While we were recording the song, George played his guitar and sang along as a guide to give the other musicians a feel for the different parts of the track, along with the dynamics. After several takes, we all went into the control room to hear what we had done. George listened intently and made his comments to Phil and the rest of us, and we returned to the studio for more takes until he was satisfied. I could immediately tell that he liked simplicity in his backing tracks to allow the song to shine through without competing with the music of the track. When he first played "Isn't It a Pity" for me, the song we would be working on that day, I silently marveled how beautiful his writing was, both melodically and lyrically: "Isn't it a pity, isn't it a shame, How we break each other's hearts and cause each other pain, How we take each other's love without thinking anymore, Forgetting to give back, now isn't it a pity." So simple and yet moving, the song seemed to take its expression from the peacefulness of his soul.

It felt like such a blessing to be working with George Harrison. This was someone whose songwriting and guitar playing I had admired all through my high school and college years when I was in bands playing Beatles songs and letting my hair grow long. The Beatles music, especially their later albums, *Sgt. Pepper's Lonely Hearts Club Band* and *Abbey Road*, were so rich and deep, and their songwriting and musicianship were so strikingly original. They changed the landscape of how pop/rock music was recorded and arranged, and George was a big part of that. His guitar intros and solos on some of their huge hits were an integral part of their music; he took chances on his own songs with his arrangement ideas and choice of musical textures; his

style of guitar playing made him an icon worldwide to other guitarists. His love of Indian music through his friendship with Ravi Shankar was apparent, with the odd time signatures he used on "Here Comes the Sun" as well as other Beatles tracks. Then there was his classic song, "Something," which to me was probably one of the most outstanding songs ever recorded, with its combination of George Martin's tasteful orchestral arrangement over his unique guitar parts and vocal harmonies.

I always had a soft spot in my heart for classical and orchestral music and even took some piano lessons as a child. That's one of the reasons I liked the Beatles' music so much: their use of orchestral music throughout their albums took their wonderfully crafted songs to a whole different level. I think I was subconsciously connecting being a part of this new creation of George's with my past Broadway career as a child actor in the musical *Fanny*, where every night I sang a song with Florence Henderson to the accompaniment of a full orchestra. The musical score and songs in the show were beautiful and that memory was still very much alive in my consciousness. I was also a big fan of Rodgers and Hammerstein's music; and that influence, combined with George's spiritual vibration which permeated the song we were working on, struck a chord within me. I felt that George and I were karmically meant to meet in this lifetime.

Despite being intimidated at first, I was quickly disarmed by his simplicity and kindness. Eastern philosophy teaches that we frequently are drawn into circumstances where we will meet our close friends from previous lives so that the relationship can progress. The soul immediately recognizes that person and the relationship picks up from where we left off at the time we were separated by death. Friendship is the highest expression of love, whether it is expressed between husband and wife or guru and disciple, and mutual love for God is one of the highest forms of friendship. It is natural and created without our willing it so

and without compulsion. It is perfected over many incarnations until it is transformed into pure divine love in its highest expression.

The relationship of guru and disciple endures for many lifetimes if necessary, until the disciple becomes fully liberated and merges back into the consciousness of God. Once established, the bond is eternal, even if the disciple slips backward for one or several incarnations—for that is when he would need the help of his guru the most. With George I had that intuitive feeling of recognition initially, and years later when I became steadfast on my spiritual path, I realized I must have known him before and that he was the instrument God had chosen to introduce me to my spiritual path and guru.

But I felt a bit confused as to why George had chosen Phil Spector to produce the album, since Phil was known for his hit-single wall-of-sound productions, including artists like The Righteous Brothers and The Ronettes, which seemed so far away from what I would have imagined George would want. I felt he was taking a big chance in choosing Phil, not because Phil wasn't competent—he certainly had a huge track record of hits—but because stylistically he was so different from George. But I got to see firsthand that George was a great producer in his own right and was totally comfortable in taking chances: writing songs with lyrics about Lord Krishna, unheard of at the time, and placing his music within a "wall of sound." That wall that Phil provided usually consisted of using two drummers, four acoustic guitar players, three keyboard players, two or three electric guitar players, and a bass player. The drummers played the same part and the acoustic guitarists would play their same part; the keyboard players played the same or similar parts as did the electric guitarists. The bass player was the only one who played alone. This was then drenched in reverb, with tape delay to make the wall even bigger and deeper. When a track was finally mixed and everything put in proportion, the production took on a life of its

own. The Beatles broke barriers and so did George. I clearly saw that
he knew what he wanted in his music, and whenever there was a dis-
agreement about a musical issue in the studio, Phil always deferred to
George. Making that decision in producers was his choice at that par-
ticular time in his career and I felt inwardly that he knew what he was
doing. After all, you can't argue with the huge success *All Things Must
Pass* achieved.

At the end of the day, when we got the take both George and Phil
liked, I walked up to George and thanked him for giving me the oppor-
tunity to play on his album. "You did well. Come on back tomorrow
around noon and you can play on another track." I couldn't believe he
was asking me to return, especially after my fumbling through the be-
ginning of the session in front of Phil and all those incredible musi-
cians. I got into my car and just sat there in the balmy London night
replaying the events of the day in my mind. It was like waking from a
beautiful dream and feeling so elated and special. I had been asked to
come back and play more on George's first solo album since he left the
Beatles. For me, the history he brought into the studio, the gentleness
and spirituality of his persona, the song we were recording, and the
other amazing musicians on the session all made the experience that
day at Abbey Road one I will never forget. But it didn't end there. I
wound up playing keyboards on the entire album, aptly named *All
Things Must Pass*, which became the biggest solo Beatle album ever,
producing several number 1 hits worldwide. This was the beginning of
a very deep and meaningful relationship that endured until his passing
in 2001.

Five

WE BECOME FRIENDS

The recording sessions for *All Things Must Pass*, a double album, lasted for more than a month. Every day, I drove from my flat in Mayfair to Abbey Road in joyous expectation of what magic I would be participating in that day. I was feeling really good about the keyboard parts I was coming up with at the sessions, and George was giving me positive feedback and encouragement as well. I had been emotionally and creatively deeply invested in my first solo album, *Extraction*, and its failure had been a huge blow to me. But I never lost faith in myself. I have always believed that when one door closes another one opens, so being asked by George to play on his entire album couldn't have happened at a better time.

As time went on, the sessions became smaller and more intimate, moving away from the large production concept Phil had created for some of the earlier tracks we had recorded. The rhythm section shrank down to George; Klaus Voormann or Carl Radle on bass; Ringo or Jim Gordon on drums; Eric Clapton on guitar; and me on piano, organ, Wurlitzer piano, or harmonium. I was enjoying the intimacy of that configuration a lot more and began to feel like I was part of a band of

truly great musicians who had already made musical history. "Some of the songs on this album were songs that never made it on Beatle albums," George remarked to me one day before a session. I felt very touched and honored hearing this, knowing that I was coming to the studio each day and playing an integral part in his first solo album. Beatle politics were such that Lennon/McCartney had dominated the real estate of the songs on their albums, one of the reasons George quit the band in the first place. Not only that, but I feel his writing had gotten better over the years, culminating with his two brilliant tracks on *Abbey Road*, "Something" and "Here Comes the Sun." He needed an uninhibited fresh outlet of expression, and this new solo album provided that.

One afternoon, as we were about to start a new track, John and Yoko, both dressed in black, walked into the studio. George's face and demeanor immediately changed and he grew very silent and seemed agitated. This was the first time I saw that side of him. His vibe was icy as he bluntly remarked, "What are you doing here?" It was a very tense moment and I wasn't sure if his question was directed to John or Yoko. But George's look spoke volumes. Five minutes later they both left. This occurred at a time when there were strained relations between Yoko and George, though that mellowed out as the years passed by. It was still early on in our relationship, and I didn't know him well enough to say which of the two he was reacting against at the time, but in retrospect I feel that he was reacting against a threat to his newly found independence.

Several years later, I received a call from Mal Evans, the Beatles' road manager: "Gary, it's Mal here. John is starting his new album and wants to know if you'll play keyboards on it." He gave me the dates, and when I looked at my calendar, I realized that the sessions were right in the middle of a Spooky Tooth tour I was committed to that had already been booked. Spooky Tooth had reformed quite a while before I re-

ceived the call and were touring quite often. "I can't do it, Mal," I finally answered. "I'll be on tour and can't get out of it." The album became his classic work *Imagine*, and I was truly disappointed at not being able to play on it. Several years later I met George in New York while he was in the middle of his *Dark Horse* tour. I was in his suite at the Plaza Hotel with my manager Dee Anthony's daughter, Michelle, when in walked John, followed by Bob Dylan. George introduced us to Bob and John, and John warmly shook my hand and told me he liked my keyboard playing on George's albums. I was honored and deeply touched by his kind words. George then began discussing the details of the concert he would be doing at Madison Square Garden the next day and the possibility of them all playing together. Over the years of my conversations with George, I saw that he had deep respect for John and loved him as a brother. I remember speaking with him shortly after John was killed. He was devastated.

To me, the quality of songs on *All Things Must Pass* was nothing short of amazing. Each time I entered the control room to start a new track, I would wonder what treats were in store. George would take out his lyric book and acoustic guitar and play us the song we would be working on that day. He loved simplicity in his musical arrangements, which allowed his lyrical message and melodies to shine through. Occasionally, he'd even walk up to me while I was playing piano and suggest a change in what I was playing; when I made the change, he'd beam back a big smile. Sometimes I would just close my eyes and take in the experience of simply listening to this master songwriter play yet another of his gems. Many were true masterpieces, but what really took me back were his unusual lyrics. Songs like "My Sweet Lord," "Beware of Darkness," "Art of Dying," and "Hear Me Lord" had spiritual messages, something I had not heard before in pop music—especially to the degree that he used them. He was breaking new ground as an artist to an even greater degree than he had done in the past, and his slide

guitar playing throughout the album set a new trend among guitarists throughout the world. He had become a guitar player's guitarist. There was a feeling of sweetness and a haunting beauty in both his personality and his music.

The control room at Abbey Road became transformed into George's sanctuary, with incense burning alongside the photos of Indian saints that he placed on the mixing console. In all the recording I had done up until that time, I'd never experienced anything like this: the vibe he created was profoundly peaceful. That, combined with the incredible group of musicians he had assembled, added yet another level to the overall experience during the sessions. As the project progressed, I felt a subtle change happening to me, as though I was picking up some of his spiritual magnetism. He saw that I was fascinated with Indian culture, especially the pictures of the saints he brought in, and he began to give me spiritual books to read, mostly about Lord Krishna and the Krishna Consciousness Movement. Every few days he would give me a fresh supply of incense he got directly from India, fragrances I had never before experienced. I began to follow George's example and ate mainly Indian vegetarian food during our meal breaks. London is known for its great Indian restaurants, and every night the food he ordered into the studio was amazing—a veritable feast. During those breaks, he would talk to me about Indian philosophy, and I began to enjoy the breaks as much as I did the playing. Although at times he could be reflective and withdrawn, to me he definitely wasn't the "quiet Beatle," as the media portrayed him. Once he got on a roll, he didn't stop talking until he finished his story. At his memorial service, Eric Idle said, "We all know that the press called him the 'quiet Beatle,' but for those of us who knew him well, we knew different. Once he started talking he never stopped."

He also had a great sense of humor. Many times as we were listening to a playback in the control room, he would jump out of his chair and

start dancing around like a wild man. At other times, he would make up some moves and play "air saxophone," as though he was a sax player in Little Richard's band. But most of all he loved Monty Python and would regularly repeat their hilarious sketches verbatim. It was all part of his personality to laugh and joke around and then pick up a guitar from his incredible collection and launch into a beautiful song that would make you cry. His style of playing was truly unique; it didn't take me long to realize that all those great guitar solos and intros that started many Beatles songs were his.

A few weeks after the album was done, the phone rang and it was George. "Would you like to come over and see my new pad this weekend?" he asked. "I'm still in the process of redecorating it but you're welcome to come by for tea."

Very pleasantly surprised, I quickly responded, "I would love to see your home, George." After the conversation ended, I put the phone down, feeling both nervous and extremely curious as to what was in store for me. "George's home has to be amazing," I mused. A few days later, on a beautiful sunny day in early summer, I left my London flat and began my sojourn to his home in my yellow Triumph Spitfire convertible. It was about thirty miles due west from London in the English countryside, and it took me more than an hour to get there. Friar Park, the name of his newly acquired residence, was a palatial mansion built in the late nineteenth century by an eccentric barrister named Sir Frank Crisp. After driving up a rather long, winding driveway past a beautiful lake with waterfalls and groups of floating lotus flowers, I made a turn and came in full view of the home, or should I say Gothic castle. It was staggering.

"Come on down to the garden, we're having tea," George said after greeting me. I followed and was soon sitting at a quaint table with chairs facing the lake. George had to go inside to take a phone call so I sat feasting my eyes on the beauty of the surroundings. Soon, a tractor

lawn mower headed toward me, its driver looking straight ahead as if I wasn't there. Without turning his head, he drove slowly past me with his arm extended, handing me a joint. I thought the gesture was so far out in this Victorian context, but I refused his offer for fear of getting wasted and maybe starting to speak in tongues!

After tea, we went inside to view the work that was being done. He was living with his first wife, Pattie, in one of the apartments upstairs while the work was being carried out in the main part of the house. The color combinations for the walls and ceilings of each room were unusually beautiful: all of them were custom colors he carefully created himself. I vividly remember one of the rooms having deep, rich tan walls bordered by a turquoise crown molding wrapping the entire room where the walls and the at least sixteen-foot ceiling intersected; one of the small horizontal lines on the molding was painted silver, which tied the entire color scheme together in a striking way. George loved to select colors from nature, whether they were from wildflowers or even shades of green from unusual plants—tropical or otherwise. There was no room in his personality for "that's good enough"; he carried his ideas to their unique fulfillment. He was probably one of the most creative people I'd ever met. He was not only an amazing musician, but an incredible designer as well. Each item, brought from India or other places in the world he'd visited, was meticulously placed throughout the estate. Tile work in the bathrooms, furniture, and artwork on the walls all flowed together and carried his creative touch. Each room wound up being a work of art—beautiful unto itself with its combination of colors and artifacts.

One of George's chief passions was creating beautiful gardens. He loved planting unusual trees, shrubs, and flowers throughout the grounds, and carefully directed where each specimen would go. The end result was both harmony and beauty so he could enjoy God's eternal presence in nature. The design of the house was his labor of love,

and the gardens were spectacular—a masterpiece that bore his creative hand everywhere.

That was just the first of many weekends I spent there, watching as he meticulously designed both the interior and exterior of the property. Later on in our relationship, we would spend hours together planting bulbs, flowers, and shrubs while talking about India and God.

He didn't like the business side of the music industry but unfortunately had to deal with it. One sunny summer afternoon when we were in his garden together, he got a call from Mo Ostin, the chairman at the time of Warner Bros. Records. George yelled to his assistant, "Don't tell him I'm in the garden! I'm supposed to be in the studio recording." That was George, putting his priorities in order: garden first and career second.

Initially, I was aware of George only as a musician and artist, along with his comical side. As our friendship developed, however, I became more aware of his spiritual side, which fascinated me. I never before had a friend so deeply interested in spiritual matters and Eastern philosophy, and at the same time so open about it. He was very concerned for the well-being of others, often taking a personal interest in someone who was suffering. Though he was concerned about politics and the environment, he was open in his views, always pressing for spiritual solutions. He told me that when he visited President Gerald Ford at the White House, he handed Ford as a gift his favorite book, *Autobiography of a Yogi*. He also gave him a button to wear on his jacket—a photo of a yogi master named Babaji—and not George's new CD, as one would expect a rock star to do. I marveled at both his courage and his role as an ambassador of peace, and was so happy to have a real friend who spread the message of truth everywhere he went.

But he could also get upset with people and was open about that as well. He never beat around the bush with his feelings and was quite fearless about getting straight to the point when there was an issue at

hand that he disagreed with. At first I was quite surprised by this be-
havior. Inwardly, I felt it conflicted with his spiritual nature, but I
began to realize that when it came to upholding principles when one
was on the spiritual path, manifesting strength was very important.
Self-realized masters can get stern and even appear angry if a disciple
openly manifests some undesirable character trait. But in the next mo-
ment, they can instantly become loving and understanding again. I later
read that to be fit for enlightenment, man must be fearless. Several
times during the making of *All Things Must Pass*, he would get on Phil
Spector's case when they disagreed about a creative matter. I think this
ultimately led to Phil being let go as producer during the making of
George's next album, *Living in the Material World*, which I felt was a
wise move.

George was neither shallow nor superficial; his personality was deep
and multidimensional. He was an amazing cook, a humanitarian, the
president of Apple Records for a period of time, and a deeply caring
individual and friend. But it was the gentle, spiritual side of his nature
that I related to most. He was my first spiritual mentor. At that time in
my life, I didn't really have any religion, having divorced myself from
Catholicism in my early teens. I had decided not to receive my Confir-
mation, and had guilt dreams about it but, deep down, felt my decision
was the right one. I knew that there was a God, but I was alienated by
organized religion, especially the guilt part of it. With George, I had a
sense of soul recognition as the friendship progressed, and years later,
when I became steadfast on my spiritual path, I realized I must have
known him before.

During the early 1970s, George began talking to me more about
Indian philosophy, which he had already begun to investigate through
his close friend Ravi Shankar, the Indian sitar player he met when the
Beatles first visited the Maharishi in the mid-1960s. Musically and

spiritually, Ravi had a huge influence on George throughout his entire life. Initially, he was George's Indian music teacher, teaching him to play the sitar and showing him the fundamentals of Indian music. But that role expanded as Ravi began supplying George with spiritual books to read as well. Of all the literature Ravi gave him, *Autobiography of a Yogi* by Paramahansa Yogananda ultimately changed George's life. He had an impressive collection of books on Indian and Vedic philosophy by the time I met him, many written by Yogananda. To me it was an uncanny coincidence that of all the books he gave me, the one that drew my attention most was *Autobiography of a Yogi*—a book given to my father many years earlier by Connie Markle, the mother of my close high school friend Bill Markle. Connie was very spiritual and offered me a wealth of information at that time of my life.

The book with Yogananda's face on the cover sat in our living room bookcase near my father's easy chair in our New Jersey home. My dad would sit reading it—slowly shaking his head in amazement at what he was taking in, or letting out a "wow" every now and then. Still, I never read it until years later, when George handed it to me as a present. "He's the real thing," George told me, and he clearly felt a true connection— especially since Ravi had given him the book initially. "When I first saw the cover of the book with Yogananda's picture looking directly at me, I felt like I was getting zapped, especially with those penetrating eyes," he told me one day.

I had the same feeling when I rediscovered the book for the second time in my life, at a point when I was ready for it. As I read it, I was transported to another place and time. Every page was beautifully crafted, like poetry. The deep truths resonated within my heart and soul, illuminating questions I had pondered over the years. I felt I had come home at last.

Even though English was not Yogananda's first language, still he

expressed himself brilliantly, elucidating perfect words for each idea. One of his disciples related a story that when she was taking dictation on a book he was writing, he used a word she'd never heard before. She tried to correct him, but he insisted it had to be right, since what he was writing was coming to him directly from Spirit. After searching through three dictionaries, she finally found the word. It was absolutely perfect for the idea he was expressing.

Kumar Shankar, Ravi's nephew, was initially George's assistant and cook. We frequently enjoyed his Bengali vegetarian feasts while discussing different aspects of Eastern philosophy late into the night. George was in his element at those times, and the depth of his knowledge amazed me. The more I listened and asked him questions, the more animated and delighted he became, mentoring me on what he knew. Throughout Friar Park were photos of the line of gurus that Yogananda came from, and many times while walking past one of the photos, George would stop and give me his insights. "Now, this one's name is Babaji and he's really far out," he explained to me one evening. "He lives in the Himalayas with a small group of disciples and is perhaps thousands of years old. He maintains a youthful body and is mostly in a state of ecstasy, sending out peaceful vibrations to the rest of the world so that we don't blow up one another."

In his autobiography, Yogananda said of Babaji, "That there is no historical reference to Babaji need not surprise us. The great guru has never openly appeared in any century; the misinterpreting glare of publicity has no place in his millennial plans. Like the Creator, the sole but silent Power, Babaji works in humble obscurity."[7]

"How incredible," I thought. "There are yogis who actually meditate, pray, and are deeply concerned with the survival and well-being of our planet."

It all made total sense to me, and over time I began to release a lot

of fear I had been living with for years, especially the fear of death, which was a big one for me. While in high school I had written a paper on the Upanishads, an Indian scripture, and for the first time became fascinated with the concepts of reincarnation and karma. Though I did not yet have the knowledge I now possess about Indian spirituality, even then I sensed that life was the soul's journey toward perfection. Slowly, lifetime after lifetime, we work out all the kinks we carry with us until we finally attain liberation, never needing to reincarnate again, unless we willingly choose to do so to help others still struggling for release. I could never buy into the idea that there was only one chance, and if you didn't make it to heaven, you would burn in hell or purgatory for a while—or for eternity if you were really bad! Slowly my deep uncertainty about the purpose of life and death I had had since my near-death experience began to clear up, and over time the fog of ignorance slowly lifted. I still wasn't 100 percent fearless, but at least I could finally see and feel a way out of my dilemma. It is marvelous that the events we attract into our lives trigger exactly what we need to work on in this present incarnation—mine is fear. But God through his Compassion never tests us with more than we can bear. I often wonder if, just before I incarnated in this present life, an angel in the astral heavens asked me, "OK, do you want light fear, medium nightmarish fear, or megaterror to work on in this next life?"

"I'll take the medium, with an option to go light if I need to," I answered.

Initially, George was searching for a living guru, whom he never found, but toward the end of his life he became a disciple of Yogananda, who had left his body consciously in 1952. Leaving the body consciously is a feat only a fully liberated master with no more karma can accomplish. Such yogis know beforehand the precise moment of their exit from their bodies and gracefully leave, withdrawing the life force from

their bodies into and up the spine and finally exiting through the Ku-tastha, or spiritual eye, the reflexion of the medulla oblongata, which is at at the base of the skull.

Yogananda's exit was quite beautiful and took place at the Biltmore Hotel in Los Angeles on March 7, 1952, at a dinner honoring the Indian ambassador to the United States. When it was time for Yogananda to speak, he talked about India and where he first found God. At the end of his talk, he recited a poem he'd written, called "My India." The last lines of the piece read: "Where Ganges, woods, Himalayan caves, and men dream God—I am hallowed; my body touched that sod."[8] He then slumped to the floor, to the amazement of his audience, having departed this plane of earthly existence. Many lives were changed that evening, profoundly moved by what they had witnessed. His body lay in state and showed no signs of decay, incorruptible for more than thirty days after his passing—astounding morticians from Forest Lawn Mortuary who confirmed the case.

God realized masters are more alive and present than you and I, and are constantly helping and silently directing those who are in tune with them. Having a guru in a body does not necessarily help a disciple advance spiritually. During a trip to India, while still with the Beatles, George met Maharishi Mahesh Yogi, who became his teacher for a while. He then got involved in the Krishna Consciousness Movement, which was when I met him, and helped support the organization in the U.K. and elsewhere in the world. The Krishna Movement stresses continual silent chanting of the Hare Krishna mantra in order to keep the mind focused on God. Over the years, I observed that George had a broad view of the teachers and spiritual leaders he met during his spiritual journey. I don't remember him ever openly criticizing or judging any of them. We both shared the view that when you're ready to start out on a spiritual path, God sends you a teacher or even several teachers with different degrees of realization till you're ready to move to a higher

level of spiritual instruction. Ultimately, when one has sufficiently advanced and has learned to control the mind and emotions, God sends a fully liberated master to bring that soul back home where He abides. George often told me how he would love to spend the later part of his life living in India, in the holy city of Banaras (also known as Varanasi) wandering along the banks of the Ganges. When we later went to India together, I saw firsthand what a profoundly beautiful idea that was.

In 1971, I decided it was time to record another solo album, which became *Footprint*. George had started to take an interest in helping me in my career and offered to produce my first single, "Stand for Our Rights," using the name George O'Hara in the credits. During that time, record companies forbade their well-known signed artists to use their names in the credits of other artists' recordings. We used a lot of the same musicians from *All Things Must Pass* for the single, including Jim Keltner and Jim Gordon on drums, Klaus Voormann on bass, Jim Price and Bobby Keys on brass, and Jerry Donahue, Hugh McCracken, and George on guitars. Sonically, it echoed a bit of the Phil Spector production from *All Things Must Pass*—especially with two drummers and three guitarists. George's creative contributions were wonderful—especially the brass parts and backing vocals. Andy Johns engineered the sessions and we recorded it at Olympic Studios. After we laid down the basic track, we came back the next day and added backing vocals, using P. P. Arnold, Madeline Bell, Barry St. John, Liza Strike, and Doris Troy. At the end of the session, when we listened back to all we had laid down that day, I was sure I had a smash hit. But the icing on the cake was yet to come.

We still needed solos during two different parts of the song. I was always a lover of great sax solos, and my old friend Hugh McCracken, who was working with me on the entire album, offered to call his buddy King Curtis to play the solos. "My sax idol from all the early Coasters' records like 'Charlie Brown' and 'Yakety Yak' was going to play on my

record? Wow!" I thought. Logistically we were challenged, and given the technology at the time—eight-track multitrack tape machines only—we had to send several two-track mixes of the song to New York, where he lived. Using a studio in Manhattan, he recorded about ten different versions of solos on another tape machine playing along with the two-track tape we'd sent him and then returned the versions of his solos to London.

"How do you address him, Hugh?" I asked while on a break in the studio. "Do you call him King? Because I have this image of him arriving at the studio carried in on a golden throne, then jumping off and doing a James Brown dance and breaking out into this amazing sax solo!"

"I call him Curtis," he dryly answered.

Andy did an amazing job of syncing up two tape machines and we "flew in" the solos, choosing the best parts of what Curtis had recorded. That was no easy task, because everything he played was great. We finally transferred the two composite solos we liked best and played the song from start to finish to see if they worked in context of the entire track. I was blown away with the solos. I played the end result to George the next day, and during the playback we both got up and started playing air sax during the two solo sections. He loved it and so did I. Tragically, not long after we had finished the recording, Curtis was killed in front of his apartment in New York in August 1971. I never had the chance to personally thank him for his amazing contribution to my song. To this day, it's still one of my favorite sax solos of all time.

In addition, George offered to play lead slide guitar on the track "Two Faced Man"—a song he liked quite a lot. On the recording session, Alan White was on drums, Klaus played bass, Hugh was on rhythm guitar, and I played piano. George's slide guitar parts took the song to a whole new level and I felt so honored that he was a part of it.

When he heard the final mix of the track, he smiled and said, "I'm booked to do *The Dick Cavett Show* in a couple of weeks in New York. You can perform 'Two Faced Man' together with your band if you like, and I'll play slide guitar."

"George, what an amazing offer. I'd love to do it," I quickly replied. I was pretty overwhelmed by his kindness in wanting to help me. A few weeks later, we were off to New York. I took my band, Wonderwheel, which consisted of Mick Jones on guitar, Bryson Graham on drums, and Archie Legget on bass. I played acoustic guitar at the time of the live broadcast, and halfway through the song one of the strings on my guitar broke, which almost threw me into a tailspin! I managed to conceal my horror.

Dick Cavett announced us as "Gary Wright and Wonderwheel—and friend," and during the entire performance, George's long hair covered his face while he was looking down at his guitar, so you couldn't tell who it was until the song was over and he walked up to Dick to be interviewed. His interview that night was classic George, questioning and poking fun at everything that was going on during the show, including his great distaste of all the commercials. I was so touched by his kindness in wanting to help me out.

Returning to London, I immersed myself once again in recording *Footprint.* I became a huge fan of Jim Keltner's drumming—especially on the song "Give Me the Good Earth." Years later, he played on "Dream Weaver," giving the track his special signature. Alan White played drums on the rest of the album and is still one of my favorite drummers to this day. Klaus provided his melodic bass lines, and of course Hugh McCracken lent his special touch throughout the album—especially on "Fascinating Things." One of my deep musical desires was satisfied with the addition of a full string section on "Two Faced Man," "Love to Survive," and "Forgotten." John Barham did the arrangements, and as I listened to the tracks, I remembered the times I

so loved as I sang before the orchestra while in *Fanny*. *Footprint* was a more melodic album than *Extraction*—I felt my songwriting was beginning to blossom. Andy Johns and Chris Kimsey's engineering added a rich texture to the entire album. As I was writing this book, sadly both Andy and Hugh McCracken passed away within two weeks of each other, in the early spring of 2013. They were dear friends to me and I shall never forget them and their contribution to my career.

When the album was finished, both A&M Records and the media were really pumped up on the release of the first single "Stand for Our Rights," especially with word that "George O'Hara" was playing on it. I nervously awaited the news as the single and album were sent to radio stations in the United States. A few very tense weeks later, I received the news that the single was only a radio hit for a short time and album sales were not there to support it. In short, *Footprint* was a commercial failure. I was stunned—this couldn't be happening for the second time in my solo career. I had felt certain after I left Spooky Tooth that my career would take off like a rocket. But my time for big success in the music business had not yet arrived—even though George was involved in the project. In retrospect I think God wanted me to make it on my own without help from anyone else. In terms of karma, my moment in the sun had not yet arrived and I had to struggle for several more years until it finally came.

VACATIONS, REFORMATIONS, AND FRUSTRATIONS

After *Footprint* failed to deliver substantial success, I decided to distance myself from my work for a while and rethink my options. My guru always said that periods of failure were the perfect time to reflect and sow the seeds of future success—if you learn from your mistakes. My spiritual journey had been set against the background of my career in music, with its incredible highs and lows, and how I dealt with it as a person. Like many of my fellow artists, I could have easily succumbed to substance abuse in the process of dealing with the emotional roller-coaster ride of the music business; but I chose a different path and have never regretted it. My saving grace was diving wholeheartedly into my spiritual path, which kept me centered despite what was happening around me. Although George tried helping me many times in my struggle to get my career started, not every road we went down together bore the desired results. Ultimately, I had to find success as an artist through my own efforts. But what he gave me was far greater than hit albums; for my spiritual quest began with my friendship with him and blossomed into a relationship that lasted until his passing. A friendship based on sharing the same spiritual philosophy, I

discovered, was far deeper than ordinary friendship. But most important he introduced me to my guru, a priceless gift impossible to value. His example was an inspiration to me, and during my own struggles it gave me the strength to deal with my career and the rest of life's challenges. It helped me to grow as a person.

Escaping from the often dreary weather of England, we went on several holidays together during the early 1970s to Portugal, Sweden, and Switzerland among others. Our first holiday was in the Algarve in the southern part of Portugal, where George rented a villa. I flew down from London with my wife, Christina, and our son Justin. George drove all the way from the U.K. through France and Spain to Portugal, getting lost several times along the way. Not speaking any of the languages made the trip even more difficult for him when he needed directions from locals. He finally arrived at the villa in the middle of the night. I heard his car pull up in the driveway, his voice timidly calling, "Gary?"

"I'm up here, George," I quickly answered.

"Thank God," he replied. "What a trip that was, getting lost in the Pyrenees Mountains for hours. I had to use sign language, waving my arms and shouting to be understood. They must have thought I was a loony." He was so relieved to finally be at the villa.

We slept in that morning, and when he appeared, I showed him around the villa. It had spectacular views of the sea, and he really liked the Moorish architecture. The white stucco houses with their bright ceramic tilework reminded him a bit of India. He spent the first few days working on a guitar he had brought along with him, sanding down and adjusting the neck till he was satisfied with how it felt when he played it. I was impressed once again with his versatility and the work he did with his hands. Rather than go to restaurants, he did a lot of the cooking during our holiday. Using Indian spices brought from home, he cooked up some very tasty Indian meals. At any given evening around

sunset, you could smell incense wafting from our villa, along with spicy aromas of Indian vegetarian delicacies, mixing with Indian ragas played on the sound system from his large collection of music. Pure magic.

We usually spent our days hanging out around the pool or exploring nearby beaches. We would even go to tile stores, as George loved ceramic tile. During one of the visits, he custom-ordered enough tile to make a mural of the Hare Krishna mantra for one of the areas in Friar Park, closely instructing the tile designer. The language barrier was a bit of a hurdle, but I speak Spanish, which is close enough to Portuguese so that I could be of some help. A year or so later, the tile arrived at his home and the mural was finally completed. I remember how happy he was. God-reminding artifacts and environments—glimpses into eternity—were high on his list of priorities, whether expressed in murals, paintings, photos of saints, his gardens, or of course in his music. He touched so many hearts all over the world with his beautiful lyrics and melodies.

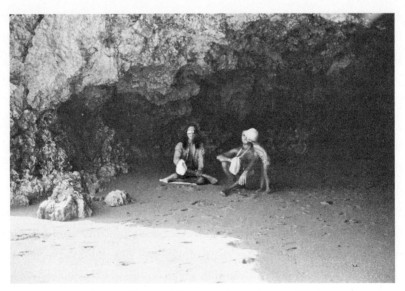

George, Gary, and Justin in Portugal, circa 1971.

At that time in the early seventies, the Algarve was quite unpopu-
lated and very beautiful, with large golden-colored rock formations and
the beautiful turquoise sea. The coastline abounded with lagoons and
grottos, several of which we visited. I even dove off a few cliffs, feeling
like Tarzan, though they were only six or eight feet high. We spent a
lot of evenings talking about George's early days with the Fab Four in
Germany, his time in India with Ravi, and his enthusiasm over the suc-
cess of his first solo album. He related one story of a frequent occur-
rence during their early days in Hamburg: John would ask them in an
anthemlike voice, "Where are we headin', lads?" "To the top" came the
reply in unison. They were like brothers in the beginning, working very
hard while in Germany, and their hard work and tenacity paid off with
unparalleled success.

At times George would take out his acoustic guitar and start a new
song, or we would begin writing something together. Inevitably the
conversation would turn toward spiritual matters—his favorite subject.
He expressed deep concern about the course the world was taking,
given that in the early seventies we were in the middle of the Cold War
between the West and Communist Bloc nations, with its constant
threat of nuclear war. "It's all God's show," he would tell me. "He al-
lows us through our free will to go right to the edge sometimes and
then something gets diffused and the crisis goes away. It's His drama
and it will always be that way so long as His creation is manifest. Here
on earth is where we hammer out all the kinks in our characters until
we reach perfection—free from all karmic ties."

Hearing his explanation, I felt fear leaving my heart that we all
might be annihilated in a nuclear war, which to me was very real at the
time. I don't think I had really ever deeply thought about God's eternal
protection constantly manifesting throughout His creation. Those con-
versations during the warm summer nights under the Iberian stars were
timeless. At the end of our three-week holiday, George asked me to

drive with him as far as Madrid, where I could pick up a flight back to London to meet a tour commitment. He wanted to visit the burial place of Saint Teresa of Avilla—a highly advanced saint who had experienced high states of consciousness. He asked me for help but I honestly didn't have a clue as to where it might be.

Passing through a small village several hours after we crossed the border into Spain, we stopped at a house hoping perhaps to find someone who could help. A woman dressed totally in black with a black kerchief around her head answered my knock at the door. I tried to explain to her in my "gorilla" Spanish—which included waving my hands in the air—that we were looking for Saint Teresa's grave site, but she must have thought I was a grave robber, for she slammed the door in my face. We tried several other homes, but no one seemed to know where her place of rest might be, so we headed to Madrid. We arrived late that afternoon, and in the evening visited one of Madrid's famous flamenco clubs. George had a passion for the music. The musicians and dancers were outstanding and we were both uplifted at the end of the evening. The following day I flew back to London with wonderful memories of a truly magical holiday.

The following summer, we returned to Portugal for another holiday. George liked the fact that he could go somewhere and not get bothered by fans; the Portuguese people by and large gave him that space. He loved unusual acoustic instruments as well—mandolins, ukuleles, Dobro guitars, and the like. While there, we met a master craftsman of acoustic instruments who made him a *cavaquinho*—a ukulele-like stringed instrument that George loved. New instruments often sparked new songs, and it was always a joy to watch his creative process. He'd pick up an instrument and just start strumming while making chord changes and singing any lyric that came into his mind. If the lyric was good, he might grab his cassette player and record what he'd just created, so he could finish it later on. He might even change the tuning on

the instrument in order to create unusual chords, which would inspire new vocal melodies. Many of his songs were written like this.

We spent several weeks in the Algarve and then left for Switzerland, flying privately to avoid being accosted by fans at airports. In the gardens at Friar Park was a small-scale replica of the famous Matterhorn in the Alps, as well as the ice caves of Grindelwald. George wanted to get a firsthand view of both these natural wonders, in case he needed to make modifications on what he had at home. Interestingly, powdered marble dust created the illusion of snow in the Friar Park version of the Matterhorn—and it looked quite real. Visiting both these tourist destinations in the summer was challenging: we had to wait in lines to enter the ice caves, and George was asked to pose for photos and sign autographs. We stayed in Switzerland for only a few days before returning home.

Another memorable trip was to a small village north of the Arctic Circle in Sweden, where the wildflowers were taller than my three-year-old son Justin, who was with us at the time. We were very far north—in Lapland—where herds of reindeer freely roam among the native vegetation. As there was no airport nearby, we chartered a small prop plane piloted by my Swedish then brother-in-law, Stefan. He flew us to our destination—a small farmhouse rented from a local farmer. George brought his newly found love, Olivia, with him, and I got a chance to meet her and get to know her. They complemented each other very well; she was also very much into Eastern philosophy. It was June, and that meant that the sun never fully set below the horizon. It went from full sun during the day to a kind of twilight at night. It took a while for me to get used to that—especially when trying to sleep. The wildflowers, the streams, the hills, and reindeer herds all moved together in beautiful harmony with the wind. God is beauty and advertises Himself most definitely in flowers and other wonders of nature. In this remote part of the world I began to feel His presence everywhere.

We got to hear some amazing stories about the early days with the Beatles intermingled with discussions of Vedic philosophy while sitting in the twilight. There were no restaurants in the area, so once again George cooked for us in our little cabin, coming up with some pretty amazing Indian vegetarian meals. He liked cooking cauliflower, which was easy to get at the local market. Typically he would heat up oil in a pan, then fry mustard seeds and green chilies. He'd add a cut-up cauliflower, turmeric, and chili powder, cover and cook, and finally salt to taste. As we relaxed, he told us about his time in India, visiting the holy city of Banaras with Ravi, and his desire to spend time in the Himalayas with the yogis. But his role in this incarnation wasn't to be a yogi living in a cave. To me, his role was introducing the world to the rich philosophy of India, echoed in the lyrics of his songs.

"How will you top *All Things Must Pass*?" I asked him one evening. "Don't worry, I won't blow it," he calmly answered me. He certainly didn't, with the release of *Living in the Material World*, a beautiful masterpiece showing more of him—without Phil Spector's production. That had worked for his first album, but not for this one. It was time for a change and he made the right move. As the Arctic holiday wound down, we returned to the U.K. digesting the wonderful experiences we all had shared.

One memory I will always cherish is hearing George play the songs on acoustic guitar that were to be on his forthcoming album, *Living in the Material World*. I felt the beauty in compositions like "Be Here Now" and "The Light That Has Lighted the World"—reminding me of the brilliance he added to the Beatles both as a songwriter and musician.

Once again I was to play keyboards on the album. Shortly after we started recording, George and Phil Spector, who was coproducing with George, parted ways. The rest of the album was produced by George alone, a good move since Phil and George were no longer on the same wavelength. The recording sessions were smaller and more

Algarve, Portugal

Algarve, Portugal

Grindelwald, Switzerland

Years after their travels together, George created a beautiful memento for Gary using these and other photos from their vacations. They were carefully strung together by a single piece of string.

intimate than *All Things Must Pass*. The vibe in the studio was so peaceful—incense burning and subdued lighting while George played us the song we would be working on that day. I felt very honored and grateful that God had given me this experience of adding my contributions as a musician, and playing with such world-class musicians on an uplifting piece of work. When released, the album went straight to number 1, although its sales didn't do as well as *All Things Must Pass*. This album was my favorite, however, the songs capturing the essence of George.

George began producing other artists for the Beatles record label, Apple, and his own label, Dark Horse Records. These included Ringo Starr and the group Splinter. He produced Ringo's first two singles, "It Don't Come Easy" and "Back Off Boogaloo." I played piano on both these songs, along with George on guitar, Ringo on drums, and Klaus Voormann on bass. "It Don't Come Easy" was recorded at Trident Studios in London, and the session was a blast.

It was always such a joy to work with Ringo in the studio; he had a wonderful sense of humor as well as being a great drummer with a totally unique style of playing. I never saw him get angry or frustrated while recording; he took all problems in stride. Very quick and aware of what was going on around him at all times, he never missed a beat. It was inspiring to see him and George interact, bringing along their experience with the world's greatest rock band. Studio sessions with George and Ringo were a great lesson in music production. The rhythm tracks were always very simple, to allow the essence of the song to shine through. "Back Off Boogaloo" was recorded at Apple Studio, a new state-of-the-art studio in London. The piano's fantastic sound inspired me to come up with my part on the track. The monitors in the control room projected a full spectrum of sound. I was so impressed in general by the studio that I recorded and mixed one of my later albums there— *Ring of Changes*.

George signed Splinter to his Dark Horse label and recorded a large portion of their first album at his home studio in Friar Park. The group consisted of Bill Elliott and Bobby Purvis. I played keyboards on most of the album and cowrote a song with them, "Kyle," which appeared on a later Spooky Tooth album entitled *The Mirror.* Alvin Lee, Billy Preston, Klaus, Jim Keltner, and Willie Weeks also played on the album titled *The Place I Love.* Splinter's first single, "Costafine Town," did very well. On an interesting note, the image used for Dark Horse Records—a multi-headed horse—came from a can of paint George saw while visiting India in the early seventies. "I saw it in a pile of rubbish while on a walk one day," he told me, "and was fascinated by the image. It will be perfect for Dark Horse." And it was.

George didn't play live a lot but he did do a few notable concerts, one being the Concert for Bangladesh. Ravi Shankar had asked George to do the concert to help raise money and save lives from a recent disaster there. I played on the single "Bangladesh" but didn't play at the concert. The event was filmed, and after George had finished editing it, he invited me to return to England on the *QE2*, which was the newest and sleekest ocean liner at the time. We had to have special, odd eating times in the dining room because word had spread that he was onboard and people were starting to hassle him with photo and autograph requests. I remember very early one morning playing Ping-Pong with him in the recreation room just so we could avoid curious tourists. We weren't following any rules, just whacking the ball as hard as we could at each other like little kids. We had that kind of friendship where we could joke around with one another. I always remember the words of Sri Yukteswar, Yogananda's guru, when he commented about people on the spiritual path who take life too seriously—walking around with glum faces. He said, "Remember that finding God will mean the funeral of all sorrows."[9] George had brought a mandolin and several guitars with him for the trip back to the U.K., and we would pass the time

in his suite playing, writing songs, and reading spiritual books together. I still have several songs on cassette from that trip that I plan to finish writing one day. Around that time, I had started meditating, having received a mantra from TM (Transcendental Meditation) earlier. I was still practicing the Hare Krishna mantra and mixed that in with my TM mantra—a meditation stew that I was performing daily. It gave me a certain degree of peace but there was still something missing.

There's a spiritual law that says that we receive through giving, and very few people understand this because they are so involved with their egos—"I-me-mine" consciousness—or thinking that more is better. George was incredibly generous, and the beauty of his generosity was that he almost always wanted it to be anonymous. I was very touched by this and learned a great lesson through it: give—whether it be money, time, mental or moral support, prayers or whatever you choose—without expecting anything in return. One might say, "Yes, but he had so much at his disposal that it was easy for him to give." But it's not the amount—it's the spirit in which it's given that counts. Saint Francis so beautifully put it when he said, "It is in giving that we receive." God knows what's in our hearts, and if we give with a sincere desire to help uplift others without secretly wanting self-glorification, we automatically grow spiritually. Having the kind of abundance and vast success George had in this lifetime certainly must have come from many past incarnations of selfless giving. Being a friend of his, I quickly learned that one doesn't have to go through every experience in life to learn valuable lessons from others. I watched, learned, and grew spiritually by watching him go through his own trials, personal upheavals, and unrewarding pursuits, silently realizing that nothing in this world offers permanent happiness.

The return passage back to London from New York lasted about four days. As we arrived and docked at Southhampton, I thanked George for the wonderful holiday—my first ever on an ocean liner. It

was now time for me to address my solo career with A&M Records. I had been mentally avoiding the issue of making another album with A&M after *Footprint* had failed to live up to my expectations—especially even with George's help. My guru often said that it's an unrewarding process to keep mulling over a problem constantly. It's far better to take a mental break and let things work themselves out on their own, never losing sight that God is more ready to help your sincere efforts than you are to ask for His help. After sufficient rest, you can then assess your situation, recharged with all the power of your will united with God's will. It was time for me to go back to the drawing board.

Jerry Moss, A&M's president, had been concerned about my making another album for the label, and I began toying with the idea of forming a group that would be my band. I had been writing quite a lot with Mick Jones, and we began discussing the possibility of forming a four-piece group with me on keyboards and singing lead vocals. Jerry was fine with that path of action and gave me the green light. I recruited Bryson Graham on drums, who had played in the backing band along with Mick when I did *The Dick Cavett Show* with George. I auditioned several bass players and decided to go with Tommy Duffy, who had been in the folk/rock band Lindisfarne from Newcastle upon Tyne. Tommy could also sing, and his edgy voice married well with mine when two-part vocals were required. I came up with the name Wright's Wonderwheel and we began writing and rehearsing. A&M in the U.K. included in my album budget the rental of a farmhouse in Devon—a picturesque seaside resort on the southwest coast of England. It was a perfect location to write, rehearse, and fine-tune our new group's musical direction. I would take frequent long walks down to the cliffs overlooking the rugged coastline, and listen to the thundering waves breaking on the deserted beaches. A lot of my lyrical ideas were born there.

After several months of writing, rehearsing, and feeling comfortable with the songs and arrangements we had put together, we all went back to London to begin the recording process. I booked time once again at Olympic Studios as well as the newly completed Apple Studio on Saville Row in London, and asked Chris Kimsey to be our engineer. The band was really tight and had more of a rock/edgy sound than the studio musicians I'd used on *Footprint*. George played slide guitar on one of the tracks, "Goodbye Sunday," whose lyrics were written by my sister Lorna. Mick and I wound up writing several of the songs together on the album; we had good chemistry as a writing team as well as being good friends. We mixed the album at Apple Studio; I was very happy with the results, and titled the album *Ring of Changes* after one of the songs on the album.

A&M Records rejected the album—and if that wasn't enough, they dropped me from their label. After all the hard work that went into the making of the record, it was never released, and to this day remains unreleased. But these are the sad truths of the music business: whole albums—sometimes creatively brilliant albums—never get to see the light of day because of a hard business decision made by someone at a record label. Acres of diamonds remain yet undiscovered by millions of music lovers only to re-emerge one day, perhaps, in some future incarnation. Foundering on the reefs of these events, I struggled to find a solution to my dilemma. I had recorded three Spooky Tooth albums and three solo albums—none of which produced the success I wanted or needed to sustain my career in music. It was the summer of 1972 and I had just turned twenty-nine—not yet ready to give up. God, I feel, was testing the muscles of my endurance and perseverance.

The rest of the band were shocked by the label's decision to not release the album, especially after all the time and effort they had invested in the project. I weighed my options on the possible paths I might take. My first thought was to contact Chris Blackwell at Island

Records, to discuss the possibility of reforming Spooky Tooth. After all, I reasoned, the band had been the most successful part of my career up till then. I wanted to continue working with Mick as the guitarist, and have Bryson on drums. I met with Chris and he told me that the other original lead vocalist, Mike Harrison, would have to be part of the equation, since the original concept of the band was driven by two lead vocalists. I agreed because the combination of our two voices was still quite a unique feature of the band. Putting aside past grievances, I inwardly made a commitment to give it my best.

A few days after I met with Blackwell, Mike called me sounding quite enthusiastic. "G"—he never used "Gary" when addressing me—"I know a bass player from Northern Ireland who could be perfect for the reformation band. His name is Chris Stewart and he's worked with Joe Cocker's Grease Band in the past." "Sure, let's try him out," I replied. Mike was right; Chris was really good and had the right image for the band.

As we began rehearsing, Blackwell heard a few of our rough demos and became excited about the project. Mick and I began collaborating once again as writers, and we cowrote one of the tracks that wound up on the album—"Times Have Changed." He was especially helpful with some of his guitar arrangement ideas that worked really well for the new formation of the band. Chris Kimsey was our recording and mixing engineer, and we recorded most of the album at Island Studios in London. I did the production work myself, having learned a lot from recording my three solo records and working with Jimmy. The sessions went quite smoothly.

One evening someone asked what we were going to call this album, and as a joke I blurted out, "Let's call it *You Broke My Heart So I Busted Your Jaw.*" There was a unanimous "yes" from the rest of the band. "No, it's just a joke," I kept saying, "it's an old R&B song title." But it was too late, everyone else loved the title. When the album was finished and

mixed, I called my friend Klaus Voormann and asked him to do the album artwork. He came back with a great rendition of an ink drawing similar in style to the Beatles' *Revolver* but of course thematically different. People really liked it and it became a good marketing tool once the album was released.

Chris Blackwell owned an agency as well as a management company named Island Artists that managed Spooky Tooth, Traffic, and several other artists that were signed to his label. His U.S. representative was Dee Anthony, who represented most of the happening British groups that were touring and releasing albums in the States in the early seventies. His company was called Bandana Enterprises, and he affiliated himself with Frank Barsalona from Premier Talent as his booking agency. The combination of Frank and Dee was very powerful in the touring world and plans were made to bring Spooky Tooth over to the States to tour and promote the new album. Typically we toured as the middle act, with two other bands as opener and closer. One of the combinations would be Montrose opening, Spooky Tooth in the middle, and The J. Geils Band closing. I got to know Montrose's lead singer, Sammy Hagar, quite well during the course of our touring together and having the same manager. Back then, which was years before he became the lead singer of Van Halen, he was magnetic onstage and fun to watch performing.

The album was released worldwide and initially did quite well, charting in most countries. We went back on the road and toured extensively in the United States as well as Europe with the new version of Spooky Tooth. Unfortunately, the album sales didn't quite reach our expectations, although we had good air play on most of the major American FM radio stations. To make matters worse, our grinding tour schedule took its toll, and substance abuse started becoming a problem with some of the members. Chris Blackwell called a meeting and told us we needed to make a new album. I was starting to get used to the

idea of expecting failures in my career and was actually looking forward to getting back in the studio, where I could once again be creative.

Our next effort was called *Witness*. The same personnel as our previous album was onboard, with the exception that our original drummer, Mike Kellie, came back into the fold to replace Bryson Graham. I was starting to incorporate spirituality into my lyrics more and more—especially with George's influence on my life at the time and the inspiration he gave me through his own writing. The idea for the title, *Witness*, came from something I'd read by Ram Dass, who I was into at the time. Ram Dass spoke about being mindful of, or witnessing, the perpetual flow of thoughts that we all experience in our lives—discarding the negative ones and embracing the positive. The band decided to use Brian Humphries as our engineer this time around, a change from what we'd done in the past. I was quite pleased with the results, but unfortunately the album was our least successful and virtually came and went. We still did some more touring in the States, which kept our spirits up given the album's lackluster performance.

One morning after returning from our U.S. tour, my phone rang. "Chris Blackwell wants to have a meeting with everyone in the band." It was Penny Hanson, Chris's assistant. I knew that had to be serious and I immediately called Mick to discuss strategy. The band needed a change—a radical one—in order to move on. We began calling friends, finding out who was available and interested in doing a new Spooky Tooth album. We decided to ask Bryson to come back as our drummer and then recruited Mike Patto as the new co-vocalist and Val Burke on bass. When we met with Chris and told him of our plan, he didn't show much enthusiasm. He did, however, give us the green light to go ahead and record another album. We asked our old friend Eddie Kramer to engineer and coproduce the album with Mick and me. By this time, Mick and I were cowriting as well as arranging many of the songs together. We were very excited with the new Spooky Tooth and the di-

rection of the album, titled *The Mirror.* We gave it to Chris to listen to, and after a few days someone from business affairs called me, saying Chris decided not to release the album and had decided to drop the band from his label. He wasn't even going to pay us our advance.

So now I was batting zero for nine and was starting to panic. Had I made a big mistake in my life not taking up psychology? In mid-1974, the band had moved to the United States, as most of our touring was now happening there. I was renting a house in New Jersey very close to where I grew up. I decided to call our U.S. manager, Dee Anthony, to ask his advice.

"Let me make a few calls and test the water for getting you a solo deal," was his answer. Dee was always positive and wielded a lot of power in the music business. A few days passed and Dee called me. "My friend Joe Smith, the Warner Bros. executive, wants to sign you to a solo deal," he casually informed me.

"Wow, are you serious?" I blurted out, not believing what I had just heard. Warner Bros. was a household name I had grown up with, from Bugs Bunny to the huge films they released over the years. Moreover, their record company was doing extremely well. "Let's do it," I told Dee. The next phone call I made was very hard for me. I had to tell Mick I was folding up Spooky Tooth for the last time. He was very upset; he had invested a lot of time and effort into the band and now I was leaving. But out of the ashes of Spooky Tooth arose the phoenix of two huge careers—mine with *Dream Weaver* and his with the band Foreigner.

VISITING RAVI SHANKAR

n early 1973, my family and I moved out of London to a Georgian town house in historic Windsor, on Trinity Place. Though very impractical in many ways, it was nevertheless quite charming and within walking distance to the village of Windsor, with its famous castle where the queen often resided. Only a half hour's drive from Henley on Thames, where George lived, it was surrounded by beautiful fairy tale-like countryside interspersed with picturesque little villages rich in history. Built in the late nineteenth century, the four-story house had a kitchen and informal dining area on the half-basement level, the living room and formal dining room on the next level, two fairly large bedrooms on the next level, and on the top level, three small bedrooms. The second and third floors had high ceilings, with beautiful cornices wrapping around the perimeters. Outside the kitchen, at the back of the house, a small walled-in garden with a brick terrace added a peaceful element to the house. I especially liked the rose beds that decorated three sides of the garden—a nice place to have lunch when the weather cooperated.

A big downside of the home was the "night storage" heating system,

which turned on at three in the afternoon and shut off at eleven at night. It was freezing when you got up on a cold, damp winter's morning, and we had to supplement our heating with smokeless, odorless coal fires until the "night storage" heating kicked on in the afternoon. There were also small, beautifully tiled fireplaces that decorated both the first and second levels of the house. One of my daily duties during the colder months was to be sure that there were always fires burning and that the coal buckets were always replenished with coal. Otherwise you'd have to wear gloves and a coat!

It was on one of these cold December mornings in 1973 that my phone rang while I was having tea in the kitchen: "Gary, it's George here. Ravi Shankar has just invited me to come to India as his guest in January. His new house in Banaras—India's holy city—has just been completed and he's having an ancient Vedic ceremony conducted to bless his new home. He invited me to come and see the event, so I want to film it as well for posterity. Would you like to come along with me as my guest?" I was speechless. The farthest I'd ever ventured outside of Europe was on a holiday once in Morocco, but India seemed light years away. Yet I could feel my body tingle with delight at the thought of possibly meeting holy men that I'd read about in some of the books George had given me, especially *Autobiography of a Yogi*—a recent present from George—which transported me to another place and time. What I was reading seemed to resonate with rediscovered truths that my soul was recognizing. Both my heart and soul began to soar with a comforting illumination; questions I had pondered for years were answered and I felt I was coming home at last.

Without thinking I immediately answered his invitation: "George, how can I ever thank you for giving me such a gift? Of course I'll come with you." But maya—the delusive force in creation as it is referred to in Indian philosophy—has a way of mixing the good with the bad, and this opportunity George was offering me was no exception. The

downside was that I only had two weeks free from the time we would leave before I had to return for another Spooky Tooth tour that I couldn't get out of. And if that alone wasn't enough stress, I was also preparing to sell my house and move back to the States that coming summer with my wife, Christina, and my two toddler sons, Justin and Dorian. Consequently, George's invitation came at the perfect time for me—a break from all the dramas that were going on in my life and career. I began preparing for my epic journey to far-off India—a voyage that would deeply affect my entire outlook on life.

In early January 1974, Kumar Shankar (Ravi's nephew), Denis O'Brien (George's business manager at that time), George, and I boarded a British Airways flight nonstop from London to Calcutta. Filled with nervous anticipation of what might be in store for me, I'll never forget the feeling I had when our plane landed in Calcutta and my feet first touched the tarmac. A strange sensation flooded my body and entire consciousness, and I felt certain I had been there before— probably many times in previous incarnations. I can only describe it as my spiritual homecoming. The colors, smells, sounds, and people all seemed familiar, as if I had come back after having been gone many years on a long journey. I had a similar experience of déjà vu when I was in Athens, Greece, during the summer of my college sophomore year. While at a sound and light show overlooking the Acropolis, suddenly I saw and heard many things during the program that seemed very real to me—as though I had experienced them before. It was my first intuitive experience in this lifetime—one that triggered my interest in reincarnation and mysticism. Still, none of the spiritual experiences I previously had were as deep as the one at the airport that morning.

The ride from the airport to our final destination was a singular experience for me. Never had I seen such a concentrated stream of humanity slowly moving through main thoroughfares or tiny alleyways. I was impressed by the ingenuity of the modes of transportation: bicycles,

Ravi Shankar.

rickshaws, bullock carts, camels, elephants, taxis, private cars, or just walking in what appeared to be an endless caravan. No one seemed to be rushing to get somewhere, as in the West. At one point, our car came to a halt while crossing a bridge, and after what seemed to be a long time we questioned our driver about the delay. Apparently someone riding a bike ahead of us had a flat tire and was changing the inner tube while everyone behind him waited. Now, if that had happened in New York City, there would have been a hundred horns blowing at the same time! But this was India, the land of patience cultivated over thousands of years.

Gazing out the back window of our hired car, I became fascinated with the combinations and blends of colors I'd never seen before—from beautiful saris that women were wearing, to the various buildings and

private homes we passed. Then there were the alluring aromas from the different food stalls we passed along the way, commingled with burning incense from a holy man performing a *puja*, or devotional worship, to some aspect of God. At times, I could hear devotional chanting coming from a nearby temple that seemed to be the perfect soundtrack for this movie I was witnessing. All my senses were working together at a level I'd never experienced before—I felt overwhelmed while at the same time magnetically drawn into what I was experiencing—a deep peace and sense of well-being coming from the very core of my being.

We finally arrived at our destination in Calcutta—the ancestral home of Kalpana Sen, a close friend of Ravi's. In India there is a saying that "the guest is God." Families will literally give up their own bedrooms so that their guests may be more comfortable. It's a beautiful opportunity to forget "self" and serve others in a selfless way—an important aspect of Hindu philosophy. Every evening, we were entertained with a multicourse dinner of Bengali delicacies, along with wonderful discussions on Indian philosophy. It was so easy for me to discuss philosophy with individuals who shared the same belief system as me—a belief system I was developing a passion for thanks to George's mentoring. I felt I was making friends on a much deeper level than ever before. My guru once said, "Friendship is the purest form of God's love because it is born of the heart's free choice and is not imposed upon us by familial instinct. Ideal friends never part; nothing can sever their fraternal relationship."[10]

One of the highlights of Calcutta for me was the temple on the Ganges dedicated to one of the many mother aspects of God, Kali. It was here in the mid-1800s that one of India's great saints, Sri Ramakrishna, lived out his life, blessing thousands of truth seekers daily with his presence. He was almost constantly in a state of ecstasy while communing with Kali. I slowly began to accumulate pictures of saints, incense, and other memorabilia from the gift stalls in and around the

George Harrison at Ravi Shankar's home in Benares, India.

temple. Hinduism is one of the most misunderstood religions in the world. Many in the West think that people in India worship idols, and on the surface it may appear so because people do have little statues on their home altars or in temples. But they are not worshiping the statues—they are worshiping the spirit or aspect of God represented in the idol—not the image itself. It's not unlike the presence of statues in Catholic churches that devotees pray to when in desperate need of something. The figures, whether they be photos, statues, or whatever, are there to arouse devotion in the individuals because without devotion you can't find God.

There are thousands of aspects of God in the Hindu religion, some being love, wisdom, prosperity, remover of spiritual obstacles, and so on. It's not necessary to know all their names, only the aspect that most appeals to the disciple. My guru once wrote,

In one of His aspects, a very touching aspect, the Lord may be said to be a beggar. He yearns for our attention. The Master of the Universe, at whose glance all stars, suns, moons, and planets quiver, is running after man and saying:

"Won't you give me your affection? Don't you love Me, the Giver, more than the things I have made for you? Won't you seek Me?"

But man says: "I am too busy now; I have work to do. I can't take time to look for You."

And the Lord says: "I will wait."[11]

The richness and depth of this oldest religion in the world that has produced God-realized saints like Buddha and Krishna is colorful, like India itself—I was beginning to see that all around me.

Throughout the years, many God-realized yogi saints have spent time at the Kali temple, sometimes meditating for hours in deep ecstasy. In the Vedas, India's ancient scriptures that are more than ten thousand years old, it is said that visiting or walking in the footsteps where saints have walked burns off karma and uplifts the soul. I definitely felt this while there walking the grounds or going down to the banks of the holy Ganges still silently chanting the Hare Krishna mantra George had shown me. I could feel my heart begin to open and felt that God had guided me to this place for a definite reason. It was also touching for me to see how George had effortlessly transformed himself shortly after we arrived in Calcutta. Wearing sandals and traditional white Indian pajamas, he carried his small ocher bag containing a string of 108 mala beads, which he counted while silently chanting his Hare Krishna mantra. This practice focused him on God in the aspect of Lord Krishna and, through mental chanting, invoked His presence.

In India, people greet one another by pressing their hands together over the heart and saying "Namaste," which means "I bow to the light in you." I think it's a wonderful way of greeting someone, and it has been practiced there for thousands of years. It's also very touching to watch Indians humbly prostrate themselves before swamis, holy men, and even acclaimed teachers as a sign of respect when they greet one another. But I first saw this happen when George and I met Ravi's older

brother, Uday Shankar, a world-renowned Indian dancer, who was one of the first artists to introduce Indian dance and culture to the West. George had often talked about Uday and how much Ravi respected him—especially since he was his older brother.

One evening after dinner, while still in Calcutta, George looked at me and said, "Gary, do you want to go with me tomorrow to visit Uday?"

I replied, "Of course, I would be honored to meet him."

All the people I had met through Ravi thus far were pretty amazing, and this invitation to meet his brother seemed no different. Falling asleep that night, I was filled with a joyous expectation. The next day, our driver arrived around noon to take us on the short journey to Uday's residence. The springlike weather was sunny and beautiful. The smell of exotic flowers and spices wafted on a slight breeze through the open windows of our car as we journeyed along the congested Calcutta streets. I feasted my eyes on the beautiful patterns and colors displayed on the rolls of cloth being sold for saris in the street markets we passed. Occasionally, a sadhu in an ocher robe could be seen meandering through this river of humanity, the sandalwood-paste symbol on his forehead depicting the particular order he belonged to.

Suddenly our driver announced, "We are here," as he jumped out and opened our doors. We had arrived at Uday's simple apartment building. We rang the doorbell in the lobby, and after a few moments a voice answered directing us to his apartment. After a short ride in a small elevator, we were greeted by a tall, slender, regal-looking man in his mid-sixties and bearing a close resemblance to Ravi. It was, of course, Uday, warmly greeting us in front of his modest apartment. What happened next, I wasn't expecting. George immediately laid himself prostrate before Uday taking the dust from his feet. I was emotionally overwhelmed at George's beautiful gesture of humbleness and respect for Ravi's brother. Tears welled up in my eyes, and in my heart I felt so

grateful, so very special, to have witnessed this moment. This was the first time I had seen this side of George, which was almost childlike. Humility is a sign of greatness, and at this moment I clearly saw what that meant. We went inside and enjoyed some chai and Indian sweets, and listened to Uday talk about his life and travels. George was fascinated by Uday's stories, while I was rather withdrawn, still processing what I had just witnessed. After a short time, we said our goodbyes and returned to the Sen residence. I never saw Uday again; he passed away before my next trip to India.

The experience at Uday's was both profound and sobering for me. Being an artist usually means you have a lot invested in yourself, especially in your career—a different road from being humble as I saw it at this particular time in my life. Yet here was George—a hugely famous person—demonstrating childlike humility right before my eyes. And I saw this on several other occasions later on in our relationship, especially in the presence of Daya Mata—a highly advanced direct disciple of Yogananda who took over as head of Yogananda's organization, Self-Realization Fellowship. As one travels the spiritual path, in addition to meditating there is a lot of work to be done in perfecting one's self. Unloading the flaws that tie our souls to the body, such as anger, fear, and selfishness, are part of the work to be done. By conquering these character blemishes, one achieves ultimate freedom from the many rounds of births and deaths till perfection is achieved. I felt that George had done a lot of work on himself in the past: I saw it in our relationship on many occasions. He effortlessly displayed fearlessness, generosity, compassion, along with other virtues as part of his personality.

About humility, my guru once said:

The greatest man is he who considers himself to be the least, as Jesus taught. A real leader is one who first learned obedience to others,

who feels himself to be the servant of all, and who never puts himself on a pedestal. Those who want flattery don't deserve our admiration, but he who serves us has a right to our love. Isn't God the servant of His children, and does He ask for praise? No, He is too great to be moved by it.[12]

After spending several days in Calcutta, we bid farewell to our hosts and began our journey to Banaras, the holy city of India on the sacred Ganges. Ravi's new home was about to be blessed by Hindu priests in an ancient Vedic ceremony that we had come to witness and record. Unfortunately, Indian Airlines—the only domestic airline at the time—was on strike and we had to travel to Banaras by train, a journey of about ten hours. Now, first-class accommodations in India in 1974 were a new experience for me. The four of us had to sleep in a dimly lit compartment, each having an upper or lower bunk. There was one sink in our cabin, covered by a wooden lid. As I lifted it to wash my hands, about twenty giant cockroaches—big enough to carry my luggage—scattered throughout the car. I immediately leaped to my top bunk, breaking the world high jump record at the same time. Roaches were still creepy to me then, and thankfully do not exist in the higher heavenly astral realms where souls retire after earthly death. Needless to say, I didn't sleep that night.

We arrived in Banaras early the next morning and were greeted by Ravi's entourage, including family members, friends, and assistants. During the journey, I made the mistake of eating some food that Kumar bought from a street vendor during one of the many stops we had during the night. Until one has built up a tolerance, street food should be strictly avoided, as there are critters in food and water that Westerners aren't at all used to. Needless to say, I got pretty ill with "Delhi belly" during the night, and it took me a couple of days to get back to speed after we arrived. But my own discomfort was soon overcome as I saw

the planned events begin to unfold, orchestrated by our quintessential host, Ravi.

Every day was planned out beautifully, usually revolving around twelve-course meals at both lunch and dinner, along with entertainment in the evenings. There were astrologers, mediums, tailors, and Vedic priests, as well as Ravi's music students coming and going throughout the day. All were part of the warm, splendid experience of being Ravi's guest. Vedic astrology plays a very important role in Indian culture. It is used as one of the factors when selecting a marriage partner by the families of the bride and groom, or even in selecting a business partner. Ravi had arranged for an accomplished astrologer to visit his home to do my chart. Vedic astrology is quite different from Western astrology in that it focuses on a different placement of constellations and planets than its Western counterpart. For example, more attention is given to the ascendant, or rising sign at the time of birth, rather than on the position of the sun, as in the West. It's a very deep and precise science whose accuracy depends on both the knowledge and depth of intuition of the astrologer. Coming originally from India thousands of years ago, it slowly spread to the Middle East and Europe during the Middle Ages.

Astrologers in India frequently recommend wearing bangles or precious stones that touch the skin to neutralize negative cosmic effects coming from potentially harmful alignments of stars and planets. It also functions as a cosmic lightning rod that diminishes the bad effects of ill health or financial misfortune karmically destined to affect one's life. After doing my chart, Ravi's astrologer recommended that I wear a five-carat cabochon ruby touching my skin, preferably on a pendant. I followed his instructions and wore it faithfully for nearly five years, after which I became more established with my guru's spiritual path and wore the bangle he recommended.

There's an interesting story associated with the pendant. A few years

after I stopped wearing it, I had a jeweler redesign the necklace and place the ruby in a gold "Om" setting, with a gold chain. I gave it to my wife, Rose; she loved it and wore it almost constantly. One winter's night, upon returning home from a local restaurant in Long Beach, she noticed the necklace was gone and became very upset. It had been raining quite hard all evening, so we decided it would be more practical to return in the morning and try to remember where we had parked our car. Prior to leaving the next morning, I scoured the entire route from my garage to the front door several times to make sure the pendant hadn't fallen out of her clothing, but to no avail.

We left for Long Beach about six a.m. and drove back to where we thought we had parked the night before. Fortunately, the sun had come out and it was still quite early. Getting out of our car and filled with apprehension, we began searching together trying not to think of the odds that were against our finding the pendant. Moreover, the street we had parked on the night before was a main thoroughfare for both cars and trucks, making our chances even slimmer. Suddenly, after only a few moments, I saw the ruby in its gold casing—totally undisturbed, but without the chain. I rushed over and grabbed it, and we hugged each other and jumped up and down in the street absolutely thrilled. But that's only part of the story. We had both been praying deeply for God to guide us to the ruby. Upon returning home around eight a.m., and just before opening the main door to our house, I glanced down, and on the tile floor just in front of me, there it was—the gold chain— perfectly placed right in front of the front door. I couldn't believe my eyes. I had scoured the entire entryway several times only hours before, and no one had come to our home that morning. I can only attribute it to a small miracle. God had answered our prayers.

One of Ravi's family members who deeply impressed me was his sister-in-law Lakshmi Shankar, who was married to one of Ravi's older brothers, Rajendra. A renowned classical Indian vocalist and a student

of Ravi's, she had a truly amazing voice, being able to sing beautifully in both high and low registers that would bring tears to your eyes. She also sang on several of George's releases from his Dark Horse label, one being a song with lyrics by Ravi, "I Am Missing You." Lakshmi and her sister, Kamala, looked after me during my stay in Banaras like two mothers, advising me on which tailor to use or where to shop in the street bazaars. It was very touching to watch Lakshmi take instruction from Ravi during the afternoon music classes. Listening to her heavenly voice and watching her humbly following his ideas is a beautiful memory that to this day remains etched in my mind. Years later she sang on two of my own albums, personal favorites—*Who I Am* and *Human Love*—adding a beautiful musical texture to my own music.

Banaras is an experience unto itself. Reputed by scholars to be one of the oldest continuously inhabited cities on the planet, I felt a deeply rooted spirituality there that seemed to permeate everything. It was here where my guru, Paramahansa Yogananda, met his guru Sri Yukteswar, and where Sri Yukteswar regularly visited his guru, Lahiri Mahasaya, before Yogananda was born. Lahiri was Yogananda's *paramguru* (his guru's guru), and he left his body consciously shortly after Yogananda was born in 1893. Many saints lived out their lives there, and their presence can still be felt if one is receptive. In visiting such holy places, one is uplifted by vibrations these God-realized souls left behind. Many devout Hindus go to Banaras to live out the last days of their lives, some living in ashrams close to the holy river Ganges.

George had given me books about the holy rivers in India, like the Ganges, Yamuna, and Sarasvati. It is at the confluence of these three sacred rivers where the big Kumbha Mela takes place every twelve years. Attended by literally millions of pilgrims, these spiritual gatherings are a deep part of Indian culture. There are many testimonies from people experiencing high states of devotion in which healings actually take place. Banaras is also regarded by Hindus to be an auspicious place

for their bodies to be cremated after death and their ashes scattered into the holy Ganges. Yogis meditate near these cremation grounds, reminding themselves of the dream nature of life and death, and how nothing is permanent in this creation. My guru once said,

> Our real self, the soul, is immortal. We may sleep for a little while in that change called death, but we can never be destroyed. We exist, and that existence is eternal. The wave comes to the shore, and then goes back to the sea; it is not lost. It becomes one with the ocean, or returns again in the form of another wave. This body has come, and it will vanish; but the soul essence within it will never cease to exist. Nothing can terminate that eternal consciousness.[13]

I'd never witnessed such devotion before visiting the bathing ghats— the large steps along the banks of the Ganges—where sadhus and swamis can be seen meditating or performing their morning rituals and prayers. The profound sights I saw on this trip to India began to change my outlook on life. Possessions and status seemed to mean nothing here, whereas love and devotion to God meant everything.

Throughout my stay in Banaras, I felt a deepening connection with Yogananda, reading his *Autobiography* while digesting all these new and moving experiences. Ravi made arrangements for us to visit Lahiri Mahasaya's ancestral home, where he daily gave *darshan*, or blessings, to his devotees as well as other truth seekers. It was here also that many healings took place through divine intersession by the great master. That was my first contact with the line of gurus I was to follow a few years later, and the feeling I had being in that small but holy room I will never forget. During the latter part of his life, Lahiri rarely slept. Meditating or expounding on passages from the Bhagavad Gita into the wee hours of the morning, he blessed and gave encouragement to the continual stream of devotees that arrived at his humble abode.

Watching Ravi give classes to his pupils, as well as hearing Lakshmi Shankar singing Indian *bhajans*, or devotional chants, I was subtly transported into another realm on waves of peace. Indian classical music is very spiritual and the songs are meant to arouse love for the Divine. I began having a broader appreciation for George as a musician for having introduced the world to Indian music as early as *Sgt. Pepper's Lonely Hearts Club Band* in 1967. Near the end of my stay, he also recorded the Vedic ceremony blessing Ravi's new home. There were about twenty or so Hindu priests chanting in ancient Sanskrit on an outdoor rooftop overlooking the beautiful garden below. The light of the late afternoon sun filtering through the surrounding trees added a mystical glow to the ceremony. The event was later released on one of George's Dark Horse DVDs about Ravi and Indian music.

Unfortunately, I could only spend a total of about fourteen days in India—I was booked for another Spooky Tooth tour of the United States. Although I was very disappointed about having to leave, I knew I would return in the future—many times, perhaps. On my way back home, I reflected on this beautiful journey. My attitude toward death had changed after witnessing the ghats and cremation grounds along the Ganges. In India, it is said that the experience of life leading up to death is a journey filled with twists and turns—similar to what I'd been through thus far in my own life and turbulent career. You struggle and struggle till the very last moment, mentally and physically exhausted, and then you're released into the beautiful realm of the astral heaven. The journey itself is forgotten, the destination you've reached is beyond your wildest dreams. My guru loved his India and even predicted that his last words would be about his homeland before relinquishing his body. Previously mentioned, a few moments before consciously leaving his form, he quoted a verse from his poem "My India": "Where Ganges, woods, Himalayan caves and men dream God—I am hallowed; my body touched that sod."[14]

Eight

THE DREAM WEAVER

was happy with my decision to move back to the States in 1974. The English weather finally was getting to me. That, in combination with my stalled career, was taking its toll on me emotionally. I missed the sunshine, and felt that England had played out its part in my life. I rented a charming house in Alpine, New Jersey, that had a small but cozy basement, where I set up a writing studio. During my final days with Spooky Tooth, I had purchased several keyboards, including a clavinet, Fender Rhodes, Hammond organ, and a Minimoog. Of these, most significant was the Minimoog, which played a key role in my future recordings and live performances. I set up the keyboards along with a Maestro Echoplex, a Univox drum machine—the precursor of the modern drum machine—and my ReVox two-track tape recorder. All together, this made up my studio where I composed and arranged the songs that became my first Warner's album, *The Dream Weaver*.

Living in Alpine reminded me a lot of my childhood—it was only a couple miles from where I grew up in Cresskill. The house I rented was one of several, comprising an estate called Glen Goin. Surrounded by groves of tall trees, one had the feeling of living right in the middle of

an enchanted forest. There was a lot of charm in the design of the small houses, and I felt quite at home there with my family, enjoying the sunshine once again. During the winter months, I spent many evenings in front of our living room fireplace, writing lyrics while enjoying the warmth and dancing flames on cold snowy evenings. My past experience of writing music—for Spooky Tooth and my earlier solo albums—was quite different from what I was about to embark on. Previously, I had written songs mainly on an acoustic guitar or piano. Soon I would see my spiritual and musical lives blend together. Truly it would be a wonderful next chapter in my life.

In my basement studio I began experimenting with different rhythms on the Univox drum machine, typically using sambas, mambos, rhumbas, or combinations of each. I would then add a delay from my Echoplex to a clavinet or Fender Rhodes and play along with the Univox. Finally, I would create a bass sound on my Minimoog and play a part with my left hand around the rhythm of the clavinet or Rhodes I was playing with my right hand. As I experimented with vocal ideas over this simple groove, a new song would be born. The frustrations I had in the past working with bass players were no longer there. I was the bass player now, and I loved the freedom of creating unusual parts and sounds that would become one of the signature features of my album. The arrangements were simple because I was relying on the delays on my keyboards to create a pattern as I played the bass parts. All this was recorded on my ReVox two-track tape recorder. Consequently, songs like "Love Is Alive," "Can't Find the Judge," "Much Higher," "Power of Love," and "Blind Feeling" were all created in this way. "Feel for Me," "Let It Out," and "Made to Love You" were written on my Fender Rhodes in the more traditional way. The overall direction of my music was beginning to feel a lot funkier than anything I'd done in the past, perhaps reconnecting me to my earlier R&B roots.

An interesting phenomenon began to develop. The bass parts I was playing with my left hand were very simple, and were not what a bass player would normally play: there was a lot of space between the notes. An analogy would be the concept of empty space in a Chinese painting, where what you didn't paint is as important aesthetically as the image you did paint. Because I could only use two hands to play the parts I wanted, I began playing with space in a creative way. Moreover, the songs and arrangements I wrote had no guitars, and I found myself liking the way it sounded, with just keyboards and my Univox drum machine. Spooky Tooth and the music I had released thereafter was all guitar dominated; now I was beginning to feel quite satisfied with the notion of not needing guitars at all. Right around that time, while I was writing and arranging the album, Warner Bros. sent my product manager, Michael Olivieri, out to my home to see how I was doing with the project. Having no idea what to expect from me, he seemed quite pleasantly surprised with the music I played for him. After playing the last song, I broached the question, "Michael, do you think this needs any guitars, or is it OK as it is?" After a moment of reflection, he smiled and said that the songs sounded fine as they were. I was thrilled: I had accidently stumbled on something unique. I realize now that it was God who was opening doors and guiding me toward the success that had eluded me earlier in my career. Things were falling into place naturally under His guiding hand.

Later on, when *The Dream Weaver* was released, radio stations and the press jumped all over the fact that there were no guitars on the record. The one exception was the track "Power of Love," where Ronnie Montrose played a rhythm guitar part only. I love exploring roads not traveled and carving out new pathways for other recording artists; and that's what was happening now. After *The Dream Weaver* achieved the huge success it did, I began hearing Minimoog bass along with synthe-

sizers on many pop and R&B records. It literally created a revolution in the music industry. I say that in all humility, because it was truly God's inspiration that created my new direction in music.

My only regret was that I didn't start my own synthesizer company, since I had pioneered the use of the cut-down keyboard for live performances, working alongside the engineers at both Moog and Oberheim. I was the first artist to record an all-keyboard pop album—with the exception of drums—and I was the first to tour with an all-keyboard band. On another note, Roger Linn, who was a close friend of my stage drummer, Art Wood, was inspired by our use of the Univox drum machine in our live shows along with the drums. He saw the possibilities in creating a drum machine, initially using samples from Art Wood's drums. After much experimentation, he created the LinnDrum machine, which ushered a sonic revolution in the music business. To this day, drum machines are still heard in multiple genres of music.

The inspiration behind the writing of the song "Dream Weaver" was truly a karmic event in my life. While still living in the U.K., shortly before my trip to India, I continued my practice of reading many of Yogananda's books that George had given me, along with meditating daily. I always kept a little pad nearby where I would write down song titles or lyrical ideas for songs that were inspired by what I had read. On one such occasion, while browsing through a book of poetry written by Yogananda called *Songs of the Soul*, I came across a poem that immediately drew my attention. Because of its significance in my life, I include it here:

GOD! GOD! GOD![15]

From the depths of slumber,
As I ascend the spiral stairway of wakefulness,

I whisper

God! God! God!

Thou art the food, and when I break my fast

Of nightly separation from Thee,

I taste Thee, and mentally say:

God! God! God!

No matter where I go, the spotlight of my mind

Ever keeps turning on Thee;

And in the battle din of activity my silent war-cry is ever:

God! God! God!

When boisterous storms of trials shriek

And worries howl at me,

I drown their noises, loudly chanting

God! God! God!

When my mind weaves dreams

With threads of memories,

On that magic cloth I do emboss:

God! God! God!

Every night, in time of deepest sleep,

My peace dreams and calls: Joy! Joy! Joy!

And my joy comes singing evermore:

God! God! God!

In waking, eating, working, dreaming, sleeping,

Serving, meditating, chanting, divinely loving,

My soul constantly hums, unheard by any:

God! God! God!

The part that immediately caught my attention was the passage that read: "When my mind weaves dreams with threads of memories, on that magic cloth I do emboss: God! God! God!" I focused on that passage for several moments and wrote down the words "Dream Weaver."

Several months later, while visiting a friend in the English country-side, I felt inspired to write a song one afternoon. Looking through my writing journal, I was drawn to the words "Dream Weaver" as a possible candidate. I picked up my acoustic guitar and began writing. Within a couple of hours, the song was finished. It had flowed effortlessly out of me as if composed by an unseen hand. At the time I wrote it, the lyrical phrase "Dream Weaver" signified to me a fantasy flight of the imagination, but as time went on, I realized the song carried a much deeper meaning. As radio play increased and people and the press began asking me what the song was about, I began to reflect more and more on what I had written—or perhaps more accurately, what was written through me. The meaning finally came to me. "Dream Weaver, I believe you can get me through the night" was about God in His aspect of infinite love and compassion walking beside us or, at times, carrying us as we pass through our individual trials and tribulations over the course of many incarnations—the eternal Friend ever with us, ever forgiving and loving us despite our shortcomings and mistakes.

Ironically, I was also thrown off a horse that weekend, and could have been seriously injured, but once again I was spared any major injury—most probably through the intervention of my guru, who was yet to come into my life. The horse I was riding was lame, and horses in such condition should never be ridden. But as it was such a beautiful afternoon, I decided to take the chance and go for a ride through the beautiful English countryside. He bolted shortly after I mounted him and then stopped dead while my body kept going, landing in front of him with the wind knocked out of me. He then stood up on his hind legs and I feared he might try to trample me. Fortunately, he calmed down and started running for the stable. I slowly picked myself up and walked back to the house where I was staying—sore and crestfallen.

After I wrote and arranged most of the songs for the album at my New Jersey home studio, I was left with the challenge of selecting mu-

sicians, an engineer, and a recording studio to complete the project. I had planned to move to Los Angeles after the breakup of Spooky Tooth, so it made sense to record the album there as well. My goal was to try to find great musicians and an engineer who lived in the L.A. area. The process is like putting a puzzle together, choosing which musicians would be best for which song. I have always been very particular in selecting musicians for my projects, and so my first task was to reach out to my musician friends for recommendations. First on the agenda was to find the right drummer—one who could play along in time with the Univox drum machine. At the time there were not too many drummers who could do this, as this was well before the era when drummers played to click tracks, a requirement that shortly after became a standard in the industry.

I decided to call my old friend Hugh McCracken, since he always either played with or knew the best players in the business who were either established or up and coming. Hugh and I both grew up in New Jersey and we frequently would joke with each other on the phone using disguised voices. So when he answered the phone, I put on a thick New Jersey accent and said, "This is Vito Scabaladeneeziato, the manager for Little Bobby Riviera and the Hemlocks. I understand you can play the guitar with your teeth. Is that so?"

"Gary, this has to be you," he quickly answered.

I started laughing and he followed. After catching up on what we each had been doing since we last spoke, I asked him, "I'm starting to record my new album for Warner Bros. in a little bit and it's much funkier than anything I've done in the past. I need the right drummer who can play along with a Univox drum machine. Any ideas?"

He quickly responded, "Yeah, I highly recommend Andy Newmark, who not only has a great feel—having played with Sly and the Family Stone—but can play to a click track as well."

I called Andy and he requested I send him a tape of my song demos.

A few days later he called me back, saying he would be happy to work on the project. I told him that I was also looking for a great R&B keyboard player who could play clavinet and Fender Rhodes on the funkier tracks. He quickly recommended Bobby Lyle, who he claimed was an amazing gospel/R&B player who would be perfect for the project. I called Bobby and we immediately had a good chemistry, both being keyboardists and sharing our admiration for the same musicians— Stevie Wonder and Ray Charles. He told me he was available for the recording sessions and was excited to be working with Andy again.

I wanted to use Jim Keltner for drums on some of the slower ballad tracks, but he was only available for one session so I booked him for that and let Andy play drums on the rest of the album. I asked Jim if he could recommend an additional keyboard player for the songs Bobby Lyle didn't play.

"There's a young Canadian kid that just came to L.A.," he informed me. "His name is David Foster and he's really great." David, of course, since then has had a stunning career working with many great artists like Celine Dion, Whitney Houston, and Earth, Wind & Fire, writing their songs and producing them as well.

Those were the musicians I used for the nine songs on the album. Ronnie Montrose, who played rhythm guitar on "Power of Love," was an old friend that I toured with while still in Spooky Tooth. The lead singer in his band Montrose was Sammy Hagar, who became a good friend of mine over the years. The backing vocalists I used were my sister Lorna, Bettye Sweet, and David Pomeranz. I chose Jay Lewis to engineer the album—his sound ideas were cutting edge and he came highly recommended by my older sister, Beverly, as well as other musician friends of mine. He spent a lot of time enriching my synthesizer sounds, creating the sonic depth that was characteristic of the album. Never having worked with him before, I took a chance, but that luckily proved to be the right path to follow. For studios, Jay rec-

ommended Sound Labs in Hollywood for recording the basic tracks and mixing, and Stronghold Sound Recorders in North Hollywood for the overdubs.

I rented a house in the Hollywood Hills where I stayed for the duration of recording. Joining me were my wife, Christina, and my two boys, Justin and Dorian, who were four and two, respectively. The mild Southern California winter did wonders to bolster our spirits, and fortunately my mother and two sisters, Beverly and Lorna, all lived close by to help out with the kids from time to time. I structured my time and booked my sessions to last no longer than six hours so I could remain focused in the studio and still be able to spend time in the evenings with the family. So in February 1975, I began recording my new all-keyboard album at Sound Labs. I was focused and ready to conquer new territories.

For recording the basic tracks, a typical session would have Andy on drums—Jim Keltner on "Dream Weaver" only—David or Bobby on keyboards, and me on Moog bass along with another keyboard at times. My keyboard parts were just temporary tracks that I would replace when we moved studios to begin overdubbing synthesizers, backing and lead vocals, and whatever else was needed. I had a microphone set up next to my keyboards so I could sing a guide vocal while we were recording. This gave the other two musicians an idea of the song structure so that they could play more dynamically within the context of the track. With only three musicians playing at any given time, with the exception of Ronnie's guitar on "Power of Love," there was a lot of space and openness, which I was beginning to really enjoy. The sparseness within the tracks also allowed David, Andy, Jim, and Bobby's incredible musicianship to shine through. We recorded each song till we got the "take" that I was satisfied with from both the keyboardist and drummer, and then went on to the next song. Usually we would record two or even three songs in one six-hour session. What I found so

supportive during the recordings was the incredible attitude of all the musicians, along with Jay's suggestions as well. There were no ego trips as I had experienced in the past with different musicians I'd played with. We continued each day till all nine songs were finished, and then we changed studios.

The last song to be included on the album was a choice between "Dream Weaver" and a song called "Empty Inside." I had only cassette demos of both songs, with me singing and playing an acoustic guitar to show Jim and David. While the three of us were in the studio, I played them the two songs and asked them which one we should put on the album. After a few moments of pregnant silence, David looked at me said, "Dream Weaver," and Jim agreed. David took the lead here in making the decision, since he was a song man and would always look for the most commercial melody and lyrical content in a composition. "Empty Inside" wasn't nearly as strong as "Dream Weaver," either melodically or lyrically, and I think he immediately saw that. Moreover, I think in his mind he was already rearranging the feel of "Dream Weaver." As soon as he announced his choice, something inside me said "yes"; I felt it was the right choice. Never in my wildest dreams did I entertain the thought that the song could be a candidate for a hit single; but God works in secretive ways sometimes, dropping a thought into someone's mind in order to achieve a certain end.

The original feel of the song on the demo was more like something The Band would do—almost like their recording of "The Weight." But then David came up with the idea of changing the feel of the song into a slow shuffle groove, which I immediately loved, because it opened the door for a very funky bass line in the choruses. On the session, I was playing Moog bass and Arp String Ensemble, David was on Fender Rhodes electric piano, and Jim was on drums. Searching for an intro, I played a cluster of notes on the Arp String Ensemble along with a deep bass note on the Moog and sustained it for about twenty seconds or so

while David played some very dreamy, spacey passages on the Rhodes. The chord I hit on the string synth was intended to be a C# minor, but I made the mistake of hitting an A note along with a G#—two notes only—which added a strange mystical dissonance to the intro. Although technically a mistake, it added to the suspense and dreaminess of the section. I left it in and it became the intro as well as the very end of the song. Moreover, Jim left out a snare note in the second verse, and we fixed that mistake by putting a long delay on the preceding snare note and recording the echo return, using my Echoplex to spot the note in the track. Our sound engineer, Jay, was very resourceful. I love those kinds of mistakes that unexpectedly enhance what you're doing!

Over the years, many fans and musicians have asked me which musicians played on which tracks, because at that time in the industry, people mostly didn't specify who played on which tracks in the credit section of the album. They just listed the drummers, keyboard players, guitarists, and so on. So for the benefit of those who are still curious these were the musicians who played on the basic tracks—the initial recording sessions at Sound Labs of the nine tracks that made up the album.

With the exception of "Dream Weaver," where Jim Keltner was the drummer, Andy Newmark played drums on the rest of the album.

For "Love Is Alive," David Foster played on Arp Strings and I played the Moog bass and clavinet, which was run through an Echoplex to create the echo delay.

"Let It Out" featured Bobby Lyle on Fender Rhodes and me on Moog bass and Arp Strings.

"Can't Find the Judge" had Bobby Lyle on clavinet and me on Hammond organ and Moog bass.

"Made to Love You" was David Foster on Fender Rhodes and me on Arp Strings and Moog bass.

"Power of Love" featured Ronnie Montrose playing rhythm guitar, David Foster on Hammond organ, and me on Moog bass.

"Blind Feeling" had David Foster on Arp Strings and me on Moog bass and Fender Rhodes, which was run through an Echoplex for the delay.

"Much Higher" was David Foster on Hammond organ and me on Moog bass and clavinet, routed through an Echoplex.

"Feel for Me" featured Bobby Lyle on Fender Rhodes and me on Moog bass.

When we finished the last track, I felt both relieved and apprehensive. I basically had just final drum tracks, drum machine, and keyboard tracks to bring with me to the next studio, where the majority of the album would be recorded. Did I have enough recorded material to form the basis of an album? I was used to having a lot more instrumentation recorded in the initial sessions when making albums in the past. This was new territory for me, and I felt challenged by the element of space I now had, which I could either fill up with music or let breathe. The second option was starting to appeal to me.

We started recording at Stronghold Sound Recorders, a studio that my engineer Jay had found to start overdubbing—the process of recording instruments and vocals until each track is complete and ready to mix, which is the final stage in the process. The studio was small but quite functional, and Jay was keen on implementing some ideas he had about how to record synthesizers in a new way. We wound up running the synths through a combination of Ampeg bass and guitar amplifiers, which were miked and mixed in with the direct signal. He even set up room microphones to mix in ambience and create depth. So our goal was to make each musical part I performed sound big enough to stand on its own. Since all the parts I played during the initial sessions at Sound Labs were only guide tracks, I had to record all my performances again, which was OK because I played them better. For me, the most

important instrument that I had to re-record first was the Moog bass, and I wanted it to sound large and deep so the space between the notes could breathe. Moreover, the drums were made to sound smaller but punchy so that the bass could speak well in the tracks. That was the pattern we followed throughout the making of the album. With keyboard performances from David and Bobby and the drum parts from Jim and Andy, along with my bass parts, the album began to take on its identity.

When we began to work on "Dream Weaver," I had no idea this would become the song that would be the hit, driving the success of the album. I pulled out all the stops and tried to make the song as spacey as possible, never thinking that radio would ever play it. After re-recording the bass and string parts, I intuitively felt that the intro, ending, and verses of the song needed to be supported with sound effects that I could create with my Minimoog, so the track became my sonic experiment. I had been a fan of electronic music in the sixties, and this was my chance to explore that interest. To the intro, ending, and beginning of the second and third verses, I added electronic "tinkling bells" patched through my Echoplex with long slow repeats; for the verses, I let the lyrics lead me to the appropriate sound—a big *whoosh* of white noise, preceded by backward brass for "fly me away to the bright side of the moon"; and an ascending modulated tinkling bell-like sound for "cross the highways of fantasy," all done with the Moog. I was pleased with the results of what I was convinced was an "album track" only.

Next came recording the lead vocals on all the songs, which went very smoothly, and lastly the backing vocals with Lorna, Bettye, David, and myself. We were now ready to do final mixes back at Sound Labs.

Doing final mixes is a tedious process. One must focus on each of the twenty-four tracks on the two-inch tape and make them not only sound great, but blend in with everything else. It's like making a big pot of soup where the chef adds the precise quantity of each element until

all the ingredients suddenly blend together, making a delicious meal. Like the chef, the producer directs the engineer to add precise amounts of equalization—bass, midrange, and treble—reverb, echoes, and the like, until the mix starts to take on a life of its own—until it becomes an entity. Mixing an all-keyboard album was challenging but in the end very rewarding, and I made sure that the Moog bass was very present in all the final mixes to give the album its own identity.

During the making of the album, maya, the negative force active in all creation, was busy working against me, trying to thwart my efforts to succeed. Halfway through the project, the magnetic oxide on the two-inch multitrack tape started dropping off, leaving little powdery piles on the machine, to Jay's horror. Unbeknownst to Sound Labs, Ampex, the brand of tape we were using on the project, turned out to be faulty. Our only recourse was to transfer all the recorded material onto fresh two-inch tape in order to finish the album—a very rare problem to encounter.

But it doesn't end there. Years later, in the early 1990s, when I was asked to do a remix of "Dream Weaver" for the movie *Wayne's World*, the master two-inch tapes were nowhere to be found. They must have been either lost or stolen. So I had to rerecord the song from scratch for the film, which was OK because the soundtrack went to number 1 in the *Billboard* charts.

The next step I had to deal with was creating the front and back album artwork, as well as coming up with a title. Bob Lockart from Warner's art department was very helpful in pulling all the ingredients together that we needed. We decided to visit Western Costumes to get some ideas. While walking up and down the many aisles of hundreds of costumes, I noticed a waist-length dark grayish-blue jacket with a light gray breastplate that appeared to be from a fifties sci-fi space movie. A keyboard album with me on the cover looking like a kind of retro astronaut clicked for me. There was a pair of knee-high black

boots that I also thought would work with the jacket. Those two items plus my white leather pants and a white scarf made the outfit complete.

Bob hired Norman Seeff to do the album photo shoot, and at the photo session there was a makeup artist who added her touch to the costume—bluish-gray eye shadow, along with some other subtle touches of makeup. Once we got the proofs, Bob and I had a brainstorming session. On a few shots, Norman had photographed me with my eyes closed, clearly showing the eye shadow on my eyelids. Bob kept going back to these images, repeating again and again "The Dream Weaver, The Dream Weaver. Now doesn't that look like someone who would be called that name?" He picked out the best photo of me with closed eyes and blurted out, "That's the album title and that's the front cover." It took me a while to swallow the idea of having a front album cover with my eyes closed, but everyone in the art department loved the concept and I slowly came around to accepting it. I had no problem with the back cover at all. In fact I think it took the concept of the album title even further. The meeting with Bob was the genesis of my being called "The Dream Weaver," a name that has followed me through my entire career.

UNDREAMED SUCCESS

W hen the album was finally finished and all the details put in place, I sat back one early spring evening in my new L.A. home and played the record from start to finish as a complete piece of work. Tears of gratitude filled my eyes as I listened to each track flow by, and I became emotionally overwhelmed with what I had accomplished in a relatively short space of time: a new record with an entirely new musical direction for me, a new fresh image, a great manager and agent, and a great new record label that was very excited about releasing the album. Joyful anticipation filled my heart and I thanked God again and again for silently orchestrating all the events that culminated in this experience I was having.

The album was scheduled to be released in July 1975, and I had several meetings and phone calls with my manager, Dee Anthony, and Russ Thyret in the Warner Bros. radio promotion department, as well as Bob Regehr who was in charge of artist relations and tour support. The overall feeling at the label was very positive, and they were ready to pull out all the stops to promote the album. Dee was flying high with the success of Peter Frampton's live album *Frampton Comes Alive*. He

had been managing Peter for several years before the album was released, and its huge worldwide success gave him a lot of leverage in the business.

The Dream Weaver was released in July 1975, and we collectively decided to release "Love Is Alive" as the first single. On FM radio, "Dream Weaver" and "Love Is Alive" were both getting heavy play and I was thrilled with my first radio success. In the midst of all this activity, which included multiple concert requests coming in from my agent, Frank Barsalona at Premier Talent, I was busy looking for stage clothes that would echo the album cover. The black boots got replaced with knee-high silver boots; I kept the white pants and scarf in the equation, but opted to copy the album's waist-length jacket—only in silver lamé, with a white plastic snap-on breastplate. I wound up having several combinations of this costume to take with me on the road. My next task was to design the stage layout for my show, including any special effects such as smoke machines, which were very popular at the time. I even bought my own mirror ball for the beginning and ending of "Dream Weaver."

High on my priority list was of course to start looking for musicians for my backing band, and once again I began asking my friends for recommendations. The band I wound up with after several shows was Steve Porcaro on Moog bass, clavinet, and Arp Strings; Peter Reilich on Fender Rhodes, Hammond organ, and clavinet; Art Wood on drums; and my sister Lorna and Bettye Sweet on backing vocals. Years later, Steve became one of the founding members of Toto, along with his brothers Jeff and Mike. He also cowrote "Human Nature" for Michael Jackson's *Thriller* album. The all-keyboard band played really well together and the cut-down Moog synths that Steve and I played were very liberating. I had spent many years sitting behind a Hammond organ in Spooky Tooth, but now I could roam all over the stage and have a great time playing and singing. During the first few weeks of

touring as the opening act for Peter Frampton, I had a tall two-level metal scaffold constructed where my keyboards would be stationed. This was just prior to my using the cut-down Moog. It looked very industrial, and when Dee first saw it, he looked at it and said, "Have you changed your profession from musician to house painter?" I laughed and agreed to lose the scaffolding. But we kept the mirror ball for "Dream Weaver," which, when twirling and lit with a spotlight, added an outer-space, mystical element to the show.

The album was released in July and "Love Is Alive" came out as the first single, but it didn't cross over to Top 40 radio as we all thought it would. "Dream Weaver," however, was still getting enormous air play on FM Radio, so Warner Bros. decided to release it as the second single. It shot up the charts like a rocket and reached the number 2 position in the *Billboard* charts in March 1976 and the number 1 position in *Cash Box* the week of March 27, which at the time was equally as important as *Billboard*. A few months later, the album reached number 7 in the *Billboard* album charts. I was beside myself with what was happening all around me—virtually coming from obscurity to stardom overnight. The hard work and tenacity had paid off. With all the airplay "Dream Weaver" was getting at the time, a well-known DJ at FM radio defined the track as not just a song, but more like a weather front moving in. I was now starting to headline my own shows; offers to do large concerts in baseball stadiums with Peter, Yes, and Fleetwood Mac came flooding in; I began receiving trophies for participating in record-breaking sold-out concerts.

In the late spring of 1976, Warner Bros., Dee, and I all decided to re-release "Love Is Alive" as the next single, and it also went to number 2 in the *Billboard* charts. That's when my life took a turn into uncharted territory. Peter's career was exploding at the time and Dee created a package with him, Yes, and me playing before up to eighty thousand fans at baseball stadiums all through that summer of 1976. Robert F.

Kennedy Memorial Stadium in Washington, D.C., and JFK Stadium in Philadelphia were the biggest shows, breaking attendance records with more than one hundred thousand tickets sold at each concert. I was overwhelmed by how fast life was coming at me. Trying to strike a balance between my exploding career and my spiritual life became a daunting challenge.

While all this was happening, I bought a much larger house near the ocean in Los Angeles and decided to redecorate the entire home and garden—really an overwhelming task to undertake while in the middle of touring and dealing with concert issues, road crew and personnel, record companies domestically and internationally, and all the decisions that are involved therein. Typically my phone would ring constantly, and I felt pulled in all directions while trying to remain calm. But the hardest thing for me was leaving my boys, Justin and Dorian, who were then only five and three, to go on tour for three weeks at a time. I clearly remember the scenario of the black limo pulling into my drive-way ready to take me to the Los Angeles airport and me having to say a painful goodbye to my boys. When I explained to Justin that Daddy had to go out and make money, he sobbed, "But I looked in your wallet and you have money." How do you answer such a sincere outpouring from a little child of only five? To make matters worse, my marriage to Christina was on shaky ground and wasn't getting better. One would think that with all the material success raining down on me, nothing else would matter, but that's far from the truth. I think she didn't like my being away for so long and the effect it was having on the boys. Sometimes she would fly out to meet me, but after a few days of early flights with multiple connections, followed by long car rides, she became exhausted and wanted to go back home. Christina was certainly happy with the huge success I was having, but she was lonely and didn't like the toll that nonstop touring was taking on our relationship. It's typically during these times of extreme ups and downs that artists

numb themselves with substance abuse and I very easily could have gone down that path—but I chose not to. I realized that what you go through emotionally ultimately doesn't matter; but how you deal with it and what you become through dealing with it is vital for your spiritual growth.

Living in this world of duality that God created to entertain both Himself and us can be mind-boggling, but Indian philosophy teaches that this is His story and that He is the Master Novelist; you will drive yourself crazy if you try to understand it by reason alone. The very nature of creation is mixed—the good usually arrives packaged with some bad. Yogananda once said,

> Everything the Lord has created is to try us, to bring out the buried soul immortality within us. That is the adventure of life, the one purpose of life. And everyone's adventure is different, unique.[16]

While all this was going on with me emotionally, I decided to return to L.A. during one of my tour breaks. I had work to do on some of the songs in my show and was rehearsing at a studio in Hollywood, when a total stranger walked in and said, "Hey, Gary Wright—Mr. Dream Weaver. I see you credited Paramahansa Yogananda on your album. Have you ever been to any of the Self-Realization temples here in L.A.?" I thought, "Temples? Self-realization, what's all this?" I assumed Yogananda had just written books, and George had never mentioned anything to me about an organization based in L.A. Dan Pierce, my new acquaintance, invited me to go with him to the Lake Shrine Temple in Pacific Palisades that evening, and after some thought, my intuition told me to go.

After driving north on Pacific Coast Highway, admiring the beautiful view of the ocean, we turned right onto Sunset Boulevard, and after about a quarter of a mile, arrived at our destination. The sun was

Portrait of Gary when he was two years old.

Gary and his sister Beverley performing on a radio program called "Coast-to-Coast on the Bus" in New York City, circa 1948 (Gary was about five years old and Beverley was about seven years old).

Backstage at the Majestic Theater with Florence Henderson, who played Gary's mother in the Broadway musical *Fanny*. *(Courtesy of* The Bergen Record.*)*

Performing with Wonderwheel at The Bitter End in
New York City, circa 1971. *(© Dagmar)*

Gary performing with Mick Jones at The Bitter End. *(© Dagmar)*

After a Wonderwheel performance at The Bitter End in New York City.
From left: Gary Wright, Hugh McCracken, and George Harrison. *(© Dagmar)*

Spooky Tooth in Theale, Berkshire, England, circa 1969. This photo appeared on the back of the album *Spooky Tooth Two*, released by Island Records. *(Photo by Ethan Russell)*

At a 1976 Houston concert promoting the *Dream Weaver* album.

(© Bruce Kessler)

Circa 1978. (Photo by Randy Bachman)

Circa 1978. *(Photo by Randy Bachman)*

George and Gary in Lapland, Sweden, June 1974.

Gary and George sent this photo as a greeting to Mo Ostin,
the CEO of Warner Bros. Records at the time, from Lapland.

Gary with Bettye Sweet and Lorna Lee (in back), Cleveland, Ohio, circa 1976.

(© Janet Macoska)

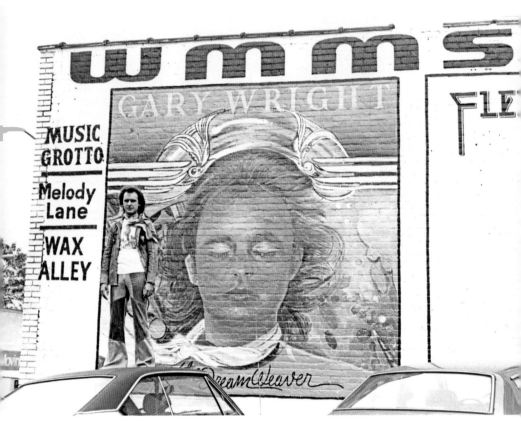

Gary standing in front of *Dream Weaver* album cover (an advertisement by
WMMS radio station), in Cleveland, Ohio, circa 1976. *(© Janet Macoska)*

Gary with son Justin (about two years old) outside
their flat in Mayfair, London, circa 1974.

George Harrison at Ravi Shankar's home during Gary and
George's first trip together in India in 1974.

George Harrison in conversation with Rajendra Shankar
(Ravi Shankar's brother), circa 1974.

George Harrison near Kali Temple on the Ganges River in Calcutta.

Gary in his studio at home in LA in the early '80s.

Gary with Ringo Starr and his All Starr Band, on tour in 2010.
From left: Edgar Winter, Wally Palmar, Ringo Starr, Gregg Bissonette,
Rick Derringer, Richard Page, and Gary Wright. (© *Rob Shanahan*)

Ringo and Gary during sound check at Radio City Music Hall, circa 2008.

(© Rob Shanahan)

Gary on stage during the All Starr Band tour. *(© Rob Shanahan)*

Gary and Rose Wright, shortly before an outdoor concert in Chicago, 2008.

(© Rob Shanahan)

beginning to set when we arrived and we entered a Dutch windmill chapel perched on the edge of a spring-fed lake that was enchanting beyond words. Through several charming open glass-leaded windows, a soft cool breeze gently blew through the chapel. On the lake I could see white swans and ducks settling in for the evening. A full moon slowly appeared on the horizon, creating a silvery soft magical ambience and a barely audible beautiful Indian raga played through the sound system while we waited for the speaker to arrive. Incense wafted through the air and in my heart I felt like I had come home.

The monk who was speaking that evening, Brother Anandamoy, slowly walked up to the altar and greeted those attending. He was a direct disciple of Yogananda and his talk was riveting. I had never experienced anything before quite like this: the peaceful environment of the Lake Shrine, the wisdom of the monk's talk, and the love that permeated the chapel all set the tone that evening. My problems suddenly didn't seem so important, neutralized by the experience I was having that warm summer evening. As we slowly left the chapel at the end of the service, I remembered a thought from my guru's writings:

> God is Love; His plan for creation can be rooted only in love. Does not that simple thought, rather than erudite reasonings, offer solace to the human heart? Every saint who has penetrated to the core of Reality has testified that a divine universal plan exists and that it is beautiful and full of joy.[17]

My visit to the Lake Shrine was no accident.

"Would you like to visit our international headquarters at Mount Washington here in L.A.?" Dan asked as we were leaving the grounds. "It's right next to Pasadena, and I could arrange for you to meet with Durga Mata, who was very close to Yogananda for many years right up to the time when he left his body consciously." I accepted his offer and

several days later found myself at the beautiful headquarters sitting on the top of a hill in Mount Washington, with tranquil gardens surrounding the main building—the Mother Center, as it is called. The story goes that even before coming to America in 1920, Yogananda first saw the building in a vision. Shortly thereafter, when he first arrived in Los Angeles, he began looking for property for his newly founded organization, and immediately recognized the Mother Center from the vision and purchased it. At that time it was a hotel used as a weekend retreat for many in the movie industry, and could only be reached by cable car. He soon transformed it into an ashram and planted many of the trees and foliage in the gardens himself. It exuded the same peace I had felt when visiting the Lake Shrine a few days earlier.

Meeting Durga Mata was quite an experience for me. I had never before met anyone who had spent so much time with a God-realized saint. A true *yogini* (female yogi), she exuded a sense that she was constantly in communion with God and her guru. She recommended that I take the lessons Yogananda had written, which cover all aspects of spiritual life including the meditation techniques he taught to thousands while still in the body. I accepted her invitation and she gave me some general tips on how to begin to meditate while waiting for the lessons to arrive. As I left her little room, I passed several pictures of Yogananda that I'd never seen before, along with the other five gurus who form the lineage of the SRF (Self-Realization Fellowship) masters. I felt that my karma had drawn me here and that this was the perfect time in my life to choose a spiritual path and get serious about meditating. I remembered George's words to me about the SRF line of gurus when we were in India together; he looked at me with deepest conviction and said, "They're the real deal."

A week or so later, the lessons started arriving, giving instruction on the basics of meditation, recharging the body with cosmic energy, and finally the Hong Sau technique of concentration. I let go of everything

I had been practicing up till then—Transcendental Meditation and the Hare Krishna mantra—and wholly immersed myself in the SRF teachings. Strangely enough, whatever I was going through emotionally was the exact subject matter of the lesson I received that week. It even gave practical solutions on how to deal with the problem and how to not be a helpless victim. I began to develop a routine of meditating for about twenty minutes in the morning and evening, preceding the meditations with the practice of the recharging exercises, a form of *pranayama* or life-force control. I even did the recharging exercises before going onstage for a concert, which gave me enormous energy to perform.

After joining the organization and receiving instruction in meditation using highly advanced techniques that were thousands of years old, I felt my spiritual life, which had been unfocused and lacking direction, suddenly begin to blossom. I took initiation into Kriya Yoga at an ancient Vedic ceremony held at the Mother Center and accepted Yogananda as my guru—a decision one does not take lightly. In taking *Diksha*, or formally becoming a disciple, you give your life and karma to the charge of the guru who remains in that role until you receive liberation, regardless of how many lives it takes. Liberation means burning up all your karma and desires in the fire of deep meditation and freeing yourself from the wheel of compulsory reincarnations.

I'll never forget the feeling I had that November evening as I arrived at Mount Washington for the Kriya Yoga initiation ceremony. The chapel was dimly lit and the smell of incense filled the air—I knew deep inside that what I was about to experience would profoundly change me. As if transported to another time and place, I felt deep peace resonating through my being as I slowly left the chapel following the beautiful initiation ceremony. I knew in my heart that I had made the right decision in the spiritual path I had chosen, and that Yogananda was now formally my guru. Chosen by God, he would usher me through both the good and the trying experiences my karma would

bring me in this and future incarnations, regardless of whether or not he was in the body. Trying to strike a balance between my exploding career and my spiritual life was challenging; but my guru and newly found path in yoga became the boat that carried me over the turbulent waters of my life in the music business.

My manager, Dee Anthony, and my agent, Frank Barsalona, were a powerhouse team and a winning combination. Dee represented Peter Frampton, Joe Cocker, Humble Pie, The J. Geils Band, and me, to name a few; and Frank represented the same artists, as well as Yes, Traffic, Fleetwood Mac, and, later on, Bruce Springsteen and U2. Dee, who early on was Tony Bennett's road manager, was warm, funny, and a true family man. He once took me in his limo to Little Italy in lower Manhattan to buy special Italian delicacies one could only find in certain shops during the Christmas season.

I also spent time with him at his home in Nassau in the Bahamas when I had a few days off while touring. Dee had a Bertram powerboat that he kept in Nassau, and he loved taking small cruises with friends and family. On one such occasion, he invited me and two of his houseguests, a promoter from Rome and his wife, on a cruise to Andros island, not too far from Nassau—a journey that should have taken maybe two hours. He took his compass reading for Andros at the marina where he kept the boat, and then picked up me and the Roman promoter and his wife about ten miles away at another marina. Without taking a new compass reading, he steered us toward our destination. About an hour later, the sea started getting rough and there was no sign of Andros. We spotted a small fishing boat and asked the captain how far away Andros was. He indicated that it was about two hours away and Dee made the decision to return to Nassau, as it was getting late and the sea was getting rougher. The Roman promoter emerged from down below as the boat was pitching and rocking, making the compass

hard to read. Finally the promoter yelled at Dee, "Hey, Dee, why youa keepa changing da compass?" We were all a bit nervous that we would run out of fuel but after a little while we spotted Nassau and were all quite relieved. Dee was not that great at parking the boat in the marina, especially on a windy day. I remember the times we pulled into the harbor and the locals spotted his boat. Immediately there were five or so dock hands running down the ramp and shouting out, "Don't worry, Mista Dee. We park da boat."

Dee Anthony, Gary, and son Justin on vacation at
Dee Anthony's home in Nassau, Bahamas, circa 1976.

Then there were the times when he would call me in the morning to discuss business and my housekeeper would tell him I was meditating. "Meditating," he said. "Tell him while he's meditating, his career is going down the tubes." Of course he was poking fun, as I was a lot different from the rest of his artists. Dee managed me up until 1980— almost twelve years—and then we amicably parted ways. Any time I visited New York, I would call him and we'd have lunch or just chat on

the phone. He passed away in October 2009. I loved Dee and credit him for being very instrumental in creating all the success I experienced in my career.

I was fortunate to have had my success during the golden years of the music business, when album sales could be in the millions and FM radio was flexible in its formats—not overanalyzed and rigid like today. Record labels also provided artists with healthy tour-support budgets that would help build loyalty for a developing career. I toured with Peter Frampton and other combinations of artists that Frank handled for most of 1976. We performed at huge outdoor venues like Bill Graham's Day on the Green at Oakland Coliseum, as well as other massive outdoor events throughout the country. One I particularly remember is when Peter, Yes, and I performed at a baseball stadium in San Diego. Just before I walked onstage, a skywriting plane appeared overhead writing out *The Dream Weaver* to a cheering audience below. When I performed "Dream Weaver" later on in the show, hundreds of multi-colored helium-filled balloons were released during the long musical intro of the song. At that moment I felt that God was blessing my efforts. Millions saw the shows, and my album remained in the *Billboard* charts for over a year. Peter and I then embarked on a tour of Europe at the end of 1976, flying to venues on *The Starship*, the Boeing 720 private charter plane used by many rock musicians of the era. Life was good.

There's a funny story associated with one of the Oakland Coliseum concerts I performed during that summer. The hotel we usually stayed in was very close to the venue, and Tom Hanks was one of the bellmen working there at that time. Many years later, while promoting his film *Cast Away* on *The Rosie O'Donnell Show*, Rosie asked Tom who some of the celebrities were that he met while working there. "Gary Wright," he said. "I carried his bags to his room one weekend when he was playing

at the Coliseum." While filming *Cast Away* in Fiji, he met George Harrison and his wife, Olivia, who were vacationing there at that time, and they became good friends. Years later I met Tom at George's memorial service, and the first thing he said to me was, "I carried your bags when you played at the Coliseum in Oakland." I answered, "I hope I gave you a good tip." We both laughed. Ironically, "Dream Weaver" was featured in *Toy Story 3*, in which Tom played one of the leading characters.

Practicing Kriya Yoga along with the other two techniques I had already received—the Hong Sau technique of concentration and the Om technique of meditation—my spiritual life was changing perceptibly. My twice-daily meditation periods were subtly becoming more focused, and I was beginning to feel the presence of God and my guru in my life. That didn't mean I would hear voices telling me to do this or that, because in the beginning it's very difficult to know the difference between suggestions from the ego and those coming from the soul, which is constantly in tune with God or the guru. But many times, being too engrossed in the dream creation of God's show, one misses this guidance. I learned that you must go within to slow down the restless thoughts and turbulent emotions before you can begin to receive this communication—and that's exactly what the meditation techniques did for me.

It's a shame how the word "yoga" has been so misused and misunderstood in the West. As Yogananda once explained it,

Yoga is a system of scientific methods for reuniting the soul with the Spirit. We have come down from God, and we must reascend to Him. We have seemingly become separated from our Father, and we must consciously reunite with Him. Yoga teaches us how to rise above the delusion of separation and realize our oneness with God.[18]

Yoga is definite and scientific. Yoga means union of the soul and God, through step-by-step methods with specific and known results. It raises the practice of religion above the differences of dogma. My guru, Sri Yukteswar, extolled Yoga; he did not, however, indicate that realization of God thereby would be immediate. "You have to work hard for it," he told me. I did, and when the promised results came, I saw that Yoga was marvelous.[19]

Ten

THE STRUGGLE BEGINS

While touring in 1976, I began writing songs for my next album, *The Light of Smiles*, the title of a poem written by Yogananda. A lot of the composing was done in hotel rooms on days off while I was on tour, or at home whenever I had a break in my schedule. Usually I would call one of my road managers—David Carroll or Alan Barkley—and arrange to have a Minimoog and a Fender Rhodes brought up to my hotel room. I didn't travel with my acoustic guitar, nor did I have the same setup as I did when writing *The Dream Weaver* in my basement in Alpine. This period of time was an entirely different creative space that presented itself to me, and it required dividing my time between the business and domestic decisions that still had to be made on a daily basis. Life was coming at me fast and furious, and at times it was hard to remain focused or even find time to write new songs. It's one thing to have a hit album or a hit song; but it's much more difficult to have a succession of hit albums and songs—and that's precisely what's needed to sustain a career. I was feeling the pressure of topping my last achievement.

Given the huge success I had that year, I felt invincible and full of

confidence, which I tried to control from spiraling into a subtle ego trip. Moreover, the negative force of duality in creation—maya—can be very subtle and cunning in its temptations. But yoga teaches that by practicing even-mindedness, you can even out the highs and lows you experience, whether you are riding the crest of success or tumbling into the abyss of failure. Balance is one of the hardest things to achieve in life, yet it is a vital component in sustaining happiness on a daily basis. Along with my elation came a desire to create an album of songs that reflected my newly awakened spiritual path, both lyrically and musically.

The European tour with Peter was a wonderful ending to a hectic year. The charter plane, *The Starship*, was like a flying living room, nicely furnished and providing great food. Each time we landed in our refurbished Boeing 720, there was a fleet of limos waiting for us, along with the press and fans. The first-class hotels we stayed at were amazing, and the food in restaurants we were taken to was outstanding. The crew of *The Starship* would buy the local delicacies in each city we visited—London, Paris, Frankfurt, Rome, and Götenborg to name a few—and serve them the next day for lunch. One night, after a show in Glasgow, I was introduced to the Scottish comedian Billy Connolly backstage at a bar that was set up for the artists. He was both charming and hilarious and kept us laughing almost nonstop. At one point, one of the waiters brought me a large glass of whiskey. When I said I didn't drink—incomprehensible for a Scotsman, I suppose—Billy looked at me with piercing eyes and belted out, "What, you'll not be having a wee dram of the hooch?"

As the tour wound down, we had a few days off in England before returning home, and I decided to get my boys, Justin and Dorian, a Great Dane puppy as a coming-home surprise gift. My wife, Christina, and I drove to Norfolk in the northeast part of England, to a kennel where they specialized in jet-black Danes that didn't have their ears or

tails cropped. We made our selection and brought our new male puppy home on *The Starship*. The boys were thrilled with their new friend. As he grew up, I reflected that I had never had such a big animal living in my home; but he turned out to be the best dog I'd ever owned. He became my jogging companion years later, pulling me up hills at a gallop.

After I returned from the European tour with Peter, I decided it was time to finish writing my next album in my newly decorated home in L.A. I turned one of the extra bedrooms into a writing room and had all my stage equipment brought in. Created as a room within a room, with double-wall construction, the studio was soundproofed so that I could work without disturbing anyone. To my keyboard collection I added an Oberheim four-voice polyphonic synth, which allowed me to play four notes at a time—rather than only one note, as on a Minimoog. The Oberheim was sonically very orchestral and was perfect for what I wanted to accomplish on this new album, in terms of texture. I reconsidered some of the songs that were written during the writing sessions of *The Dream Weaver* album, like "Empty Inside," "Silent Fury," "Child of Light," and "Are You Weepin'," and decided to put them on the album. Combining these with songs I'd written or half written while on the road, along with new material I wrote in my home studio, I was ready to start recording at Sound Labs once again. My vision for the album was to combine the feelings of expansiveness and beauty from the music I had heard at Ravi's home in India with my continuing experimentation with electronic musical textures. Lyrically, I dipped into the well of Yogananda's beautiful writings for my inspiration.

Once again Jay Lewis engineered the album, but this time we recorded all the overdubs at United Western Recorders in Hollywood and then did the final mixes back at Sound Labs. I used Art Wood, Steve Porcaro, and Peter Reilich from my road band on some of the tracks, and once again Jim Keltner on drums and David Foster on keyboards

on the rest of the album. David was largely responsible for the beautiful orchestral arrangements on songs like "Time Machine," "I Am the Sky," "Who Am I," and "The Light of Smiles." I used the same backing vocalists as on *The Dream Weaver* album, namely my sister Lorna Wright, Bettye Sweet, and David Pomeranz. One of my favorite parts of the album were the three tracks "Time Machine," "I Am the Sky," and "Who Am I," which were all linked together as one song. "I Am the Sky" was a chant written by my guru, and I had my son Justin sing it. He was only five at the time and his voice added an element of purity and innocence to the spacey production. The lyrics of the three songs alluded to the soul's journey through lifetimes, searching for its ultimate identity. In retrospect, *The Light of Smiles* is one of my favorite albums because of its spiritual nature both sonically and lyrically.

Dee and Frank wanted me to start headlining my own shows to promote my new album, rather than being once again part of a package. I was thrilled because I'd always wanted to have my own production, including sound and lights along with rear-projected films on a screen at the back of the stage. I was a big fan of Pink Floyd's stage productions, and now I was getting my own chance to be creative. Looking for elements I could put together to create these minifilms that would play during key parts of my show, I began to brainstorm. Laserium, the place to go for concert-quality laser shows, had been using "Dream Weaver" as a featured part of their show at the Griffith Observatory in Los Angeles, as well as other locations in the United States. I contacted them about filming some of their images to use during my show and they were very helpful and cooperative. After several creative sessions, I transferred about three dozen different swirling laser images onto 16 mm film stock to store in my cosmic spice rack for future use in my show.

George had once mentioned to me that I should call a photographer friend of his, Henry Grossman, who had photographed the Ken-

nedys and the Beatles, to name just a few. Henry lived in New York, and during one of my trips there I called him and arranged a meeting. He was charming beyond words, and when I explained to him what I was doing with my live show, he immediately suggested I contact his artist friend Jonathan Meader, who lived in Washington, D.C. It so happened that I had a concert there a few days later, and I called Jonathan upon my arrival in D.C. to arrange a meeting to see his work. A true artist, he had fashioned his brick row house to be the perfect home for his imaginative works that were displayed throughout its cozy rooms. His art seemed to be the perfect visual partner for my music—especially my new album.

His images were spiritual, warm, and at times spacey, using unicorns and pet lions or flying turtles sailing through distant galaxies. Some were surrealistic, like his work of a room with an open door revealing a tropical beach outside and an ascending winding staircase. As the winding staircase ascended, it faded into the universe. I was mesmerized by what I saw. He graciously offered to let me use his images as one of the elements in my films for my live show—another ingredient added to the cosmic spice rack. To this day I still have his images displayed throughout my home, and he remains a dear friend of mine. His images were used as cover artwork for my two albums, *The Right Place* and *Human Love*. It was also through Jonathan that I found John Silletto, the artist who painted my portrait for the front cover of *The Light of Smiles*. I liked his work so much that I decided to use one of his previously painted images for the back cover as well. When I showed Dee the artwork for the album, he opened his eyes wide, jerked his head back, and blurted out, "What kind of cockamamy cover is this? You can't even read your name." In retrospect he was right, but I had to learn from my own mistakes.

Focusing on the production of my live show while waiting for the album to be released, I created and assembled several films consisting

With Jonathan Meader on Catalina Island,
California, circa 1977.

of lasers, Jonathan's images, photographs, and other bits and pieces
that were edited to the songs I would use. The films were to be
rear-projected onto a large circular screen hanging at the back of the
stage, behind the drummer. What worked best for me visually and
sonically, and what I wound up using, were "Dream Weaver," "Time
Machine," "I Am the Sky," and "Who Am I." My drummer Art Wood
played to a click track so that the images would change along with the
music—a technical challenge in those days. After extensive rehearsals,
we packed everything up into two semis to begin *The Light of Smiles*
tour in 1977.

Confidence and quick success can be dangerous things if not tem-
pered by caution and circumspection. When the album was released in
1977, I got a call from one of the head radio promotion people at War-
ner Bros. saying the length of the single, "Water Sign," was too long for

Top 40 radio, and that we would have to edit it down to under three minutes or choose another track. Rather than following my instinct and insisting on releasing "Water Sign" in spite of its length, I chose another track, "Phantom Rider," thinking that anything I released would be hugely successful. That smug decision proved disastrous and "Phantom Rider" only got to number 43 on the *Billboard* charts. Unfortunately, it took the momentum out of the release of the album, which barely achieved gold status compared to multiplatinum *The Dream Weaver.* I was devastated. And to add to the stress, this was all happening during my first headlining tour, which had its own set of problems with personnel and spiraling tour costs.

In addition, my marriage was coming apart at the seams. Christina and I were only in our midtwenties when we got married, and really didn't know who we were as people. As we both grew older, we realized we weren't compatible enough to spend the rest of our lives together and decided to divorce after a trial separation. Initially, we were at odds, but as time passed we forgave each other and put the past behind us for the sake of our children. Now we are friends. It is said that the two most stressful experiences a man goes through in life are a divorce and loss of job. I was experiencing both at the same time. God, I felt, was testing my strength and endurance, and I often contemplated the wisdom of a passage by Yogananda's guru, Sri Yukteswar, in *Autobiography of a Yogi*: "Pain and pleasure are transitory; endure all dualities with calmness."[20] Alas, that state of consciousness was well beyond my reach then, but I moved on with all the strength I could muster.

Throughout creation there is adversity as well as happiness, two opposing states of consciousness in this world of duality. Science teaches that friction is an integral part of growth and that life cannot thrive without it. Darwin alluded to this with his concept of natural selection, or what we call "survival of the fittest." We find it in our own lives as

well, especially when we are struggling to find peace and balance within. Yogananda once wrote,

> Use every trial that comes to you as an opportunity to improve yourself. When you are passing through the difficulties and tests of life, you usually become rebellious: "Why should this happen to me?" Instead, you should think of every trial as a pickax with which to dig into the soil of your consciousness and release the fountain of spiritual strength that lies within. Each test should bring out the hidden power that is within you as a child of God, made in His image.[21]

As *The Light of Smiles* tour wound down, my spiritual batteries had been running low and needed recharging. I had been working almost nonstop for nearly three years and was glad to be going home to regroup and take a break from my career. Deep down I was also really looking forward to visiting the Mother Center and going to the weekly lectures at the Lake Shrine Temple in Pacific Palisades. Shortly after I arrived back in L.A., I drove to the temple for the Thursday night service. As I walked into the Windmill Chapel I paused just inside the doorway, overwhelmed by waves of love emanating from my guru's photo on the altar. As has happened many times since that night, the talk that evening seemed to be directed right at me. It was almost like having the guru right there giving me a pep talk. He once said,

> Though your errors be as deep as the ocean, the soul itself cannot be swallowed up by them. Have unflinching determination to move on your path unhampered by limiting thoughts of past errors.[22]

> The root of sorrow lies in the dearth of heroism and courage in the character of the average man. When the heroic element is lacking in

the mental makeup of a person, his mind becomes susceptible to the threat of all passing sorrows.[23]

As I left the beautiful chapel that evening, I resolved to be more positive in my outlook both in my career and family life, in spite of outside circumstances. I felt my guru would guide me through this stormy episode.

I had outgrown my small writing room, and decided it was time to start building a recording studio in my home. Using the same room, I modified it and made it a soundproof overdubbing room, with nonparallel wall surfaces to prevent alteration of the sound of the room itself. The idea was that the recorded music should sound the same anywhere and on any system it was played on—that is, exactly as it did in my studio when it was first recorded. I also bought a multitrack tape machine for recording my synthesizers, which had grown in number since finishing the last tour.

I changed my approach to songwriting for the new album, which I named *Touch and Gone*. Of the nine tracks that made it to the album, six were cowritten with other writers, a new approach for me. *The Dream Weaver* only had one co-written song, as did *The Light of Smiles*. Looking back, I think I lost confidence after the failure of the last album and felt that adding new writers might bring some fresh ideas to my music. In retrospect, I think that was a mistake: I was diluting the gift I had been given. There is something special that occurs when an artist sings the words and melodies he or she wrote, exposing a part of his or her soul.

Adding another new element, I used Matthew Hyde as my engineer and once again recorded the basic tracks and did the final mixing at Sound Labs. All the overdubs, including my synths and vocals, were done in my home studio. The musicians I used were from my live band,

with the exception of Bobby Lyle: Art Wood on drums, Richard Baker, Peter Reilich, Gary Mielke, and Hiroshi Upshur on keyboards. Again, I played the Moog bass, solos, and other synth parts throughout the album. When it was mixed and ready for release, I wasn't quite sure whether it was up to par with my two previous albums. Although I tried to remain positive, I began to harbor doubts. Recruiting band members, we started rehearsals for an upcoming tour to support release of the record. For the production, I created and added more films from tracks on the new album, along with material I used from *The Light of Smiles* tour.

The tour started in the fall of 1977, along with the release of the first single, "Touch and Gone," which unfortunately reached only number 117 in the *Billboard* charts. My manager, Dee, told me confidentially that Warner Bros. wasn't very excited about the album, feeling there were no hit singles, and that translated into only modest success at radio and retail. Things seemed to be going from bad to worse. I had to cancel the rest of the tour due to weak sales at the box office. Fear was starting to creep in; only two albums ago I was riding the crest of a huge wave of success, and now it all seemed to be coming apart. Was this what was left of my career? Yogananda often said that dwelling on problems constantly is not psychologically healthy. It's best sometimes to take a break from life, to let things work themselves out while focusing on thoughts of success and hanging out with positive, uplifting people. Thoughts are like magnets, and can draw the very things you constantly think about.

But the season of failure can sometimes be the best time to sow the seeds of success. I've never been one for giving up and being resigned to so-called "fate," which really doesn't exist. Karma brought over from the past definitely has an influence on the events of one's life, but that too can be mitigated by meditation and right action. Taking psychological inventory and dispassionately looking at mistakes in the

decision-making process can prevent repetition of failure. I made the decision that I was going to stop touring until I had another successful album that would justify my going out on the road to support the release. Fear had paralyzed my creative efforts on *Touch and Gone*, resulting in my being overinfluenced by currently successful albums. I remember Leon Russell once telling me that if you chase trends, you'll always be behind, trying to catch up. A far better course lies in setting the trends, which I believe I did with *The Dream Weaver*. It was time for me to climb into the helicopter of self-analysis and view the trend of my life from a different perspective. What better place to do that than in India.

I RETURN TO INDIA

met my dear friend Chris Agajanian through my tour manager, Ron Nehoda, while on a break from *The Dream Weaver* album tour. Ron had met Chris at a Stephen Stills party after a Peter Frampton concert in Los Angeles in 1976. Chris and Stephen both shared an interest in racing cars, and Chris's dad, J. C. Agajanian, was involved early on with the Indy 500. Both he and his family won three races over six different decades. The family were also the owners and operators of the well-known Ascot Park Raceway in L.A. We became good friends over the next few years; he was always positive and highly motivated, and I liked his energy. He was also very interested in the spiritual part of my life and we frequently entered into deep discussions about metaphysics and religion. I asked him if he wanted to come to India with me. After a moment of reflection, he smiled and said, "India? Wow, I would love to go to India."

In April 1978, we arrived in Bombay after what seemed to be a 24-hour flight, if you added up all the layovers. George had always advised me to stay away from the big cities when traveling in India and to concentrate on the holy places and pilgrimage spots, which to me were the

essence of India's beauty. We spent six weeks visiting places I didn't get to see on my first trip with George—Kashmir, Haridwar, Rishikesh, Agra, and Kathmandu in Nepal, to name a few—but also Calcutta and Banaras because of their connection with Yogananda's early life. I wanted to make this trip a personal pilgrimage, visiting the places where my guru had played out his early role as a God-realized master. Chris graciously went along with the program, filming the sights and people as we went along.

After spending the first night at a hotel near the Bombay airport, we flew to Calcutta the next day. I remember the feeling I had had when landing there four years earlier with George, and now once again a deep sense of belonging radiated through me as we walked through the terminal. I felt Mother India embracing me once again. The worries of my career now seemed thousands of miles away, their importance replaced by a beautiful sense of peacefulness—the life and breath of this land and home of the Vedas, sacred scriptures written thousands of years ago yet still relevant.

While in Calcutta, I particularly wanted to visit my guru's home on 4 Garpar Road, where God in the aspect of the Divine Mother first revealed Herself to young Yogananda in his tiny attic room where he regularly meditated—sometimes into the wee hours of the morning. It was also here where the God-realized Mahavatar Babaji paid my guru a visit just before he left for Boston in 1920. The incident was described by Yogananda in his book *Autobiography of a Yogi*. Waiting for a sign after spending hours deeply praying for divine permission to go to America, he says,

> I felt that if I cried once more, increasing the depth of my inner passion, my brain would split. At that moment there came a knock on the door of my Garpar Road home. Answering the summons, I beheld a young man in the scanty garb of a renunciant. He entered the house.

"He must be Babaji!". . . . He answered my thought. "Yes, I am Babaji. . . . Our Heavenly Father has heard your prayer. He commands me to tell you: Follow the behests of your guru and go to America. Fear not; you shall be protected."[24]

After settling into our hotel and trying to catch up on lost sleep, we finally got up, had a meal, and arranged for a car to drive us to Garpar Road. We had previously contacted the Yogoda Satsanga Society—SRF's organizational name in India—to arrange for someone meet us at the Garpar home. I was overcome with joyous anticipation as we drove toward our destination. Chris was busy taking in the array of sights, sounds, and pungent aromas as we meandered down the colorful, noisy streets toward our destination. Our driver slowed down and came to a sudden stop in front of the house and Chris and I walked up to the front door and rang the bell. The door opened and a tall regal-looking man who bore an incredible resemblance to Yogananda greeted us. It was my guru's younger brother, Sananda Lal Ghosh—charming and gracious as well as being a talented artist. After serving us chai and some Bengali pastries, he escorted us to the tiny attic meditation room I had so anxiously waited to see and invited us to sit for a short meditation. The blissful vibrations left behind by my guru in that tiny room were uplifting beyond words. After a few moments of silence, Sananda motioned us to follow him down a flight of stairs to the room where Mahavatar Babaji had paid a visit. He was an incarnation of love, and I was engulfed in the blessings he'd left behind.

Downstairs we went to the dining area, where more chai and Indian sweetmeats were served. Sananda was a great storyteller, and when probed a bit to share some of his experiences with his yogi brother and spiritual family, he humbly consented. Our father, Bhagabati Charan Ghosh, was also an advanced Kriya Yogi and a disciple of Lahiri Mahasaya. One afternoon, while the family was still living at home, Father

began to experience great discomfort in his body and finally called for the family doctor. He was diagnosed with appendicitis and had to have emergency surgery. Requesting that the doctor perform the operation right there in his kitchen, he refused any anesthetic and began to meditate, instructing the doctor to begin the surgery when he raised his right index finger. He never moved during the entire surgery. Needless to say, the doctor was dumbfounded at what he saw.

Sananda further related that another incident occurred when Yogananda returned to India in 1936, at the behest of his saintly guru Swami Sri Yukteswar. Sananda was one of the designated drivers while his yogi brother toured India, giving lectures and meeting saints that were to be included in his yet-to-be-written book, *Autobiography of a Yogi*. One such occasion involved meeting the highly advanced *yogini* saint, Ananda Moyi Ma, who was visiting Calcutta at the time. About their first meeting, Yogananda wrote,

> We sat together in the rear seats of the car. The Blissful Mother soon entered the immobile ecstatic state. Her beautiful eyes glanced heavenward and, half-opened, became stilled, gazing into the near-far inner Elysium. . . . I had found many men of God-realization in India, but never before had I met such an exalted woman saint. Her gentle face was burnished with the ineffable joy that had given her the name of Blissful Mother.[25]

Sananda told me that Yogananda had invited Ananda Moyi Ma to visit his ashram in Ranchi—a very long drive from Jamshedpur, where she was staying at the time with several of her devotees. Upon arriving in Ranchi that afternoon, a sumptuous feast was prepared in celebration of her visit. But as evening approached, several of her accompanying disciples expressed a desire to return home that evening with Ma. Not having slept for two days after all the driving, Sananda was con-

cerned about the safety of such a long trip at night, but his brother as-
sured him that with Ma in the car he would be safe—even though part
of the journey was through winding mountain roads inhabited by
bears and tigers. Several hours after their departure, and upon entering
the mountain pass, he realized that he had forgotten to fill the car with
gasoline before leaving Ranchi—it registered empty on the fuel gauge.
Coasting downhill while turning the engine off to save on gas, they
finally reached a gas station and discovered that the fuel tank was bone
dry and that they had driven the long distance on an empty tank—a
miracle no doubt humbly set in motion through the grace of Ananda
Moyi Ma.

We bid Sananda farewell and prepared to leave for Kathmandu and
the kingdom of Nepal the next day. Flying over the nearly five-mile-
high Himalayas was a beautiful experience; Indian scripture is rich with
stories of the sacred mountain range as the source of the holy Ganges.
We arrived in the capital, Kathmandu, a colorful and spiritual small
city with many Buddhist and Hindu temples. After a few days of sight-
seeing, we hired a car and drove about 120 miles west to visit Pokhara
Valley—breathtaking and surrounded by a dramatic part of the Hima-
layan range and one of the world's highest mountains, Annapurna.
Returning to Kathmandu to do some last-minute shopping, we then
departed for Banaras to continue our spiritual pilgrimage.

Chris was very touched by the holiness of Banaras. Watching the
daily prayer offerings floating down the Ganges, the yogis, sadhus,
and swamis performing sunrise *puja* ceremonies on the steps of the
ghats, all set against the backdrop of temples perhaps thousands of
years old and perched over the sacred river, even slightly tilted with
age—these images together added to the profound sense of spirituality
that was once again waking in me since my last visit with George.
Chris felt it as well. We made arrangements with the Lahiri family to

visit the ancestral home of my *paramguru*'s guru, Lahiri Mahasaya. Entering the small room where he blessed and initiated devotees into Kriya Yoga, I felt his blissful vibrations filling my consciousness. Since having been there with George and Ravi in 1974, I was now for the first time experiencing Lahiri's presence as a devotee connected to a line of God-realized masters: Babaji, Lahiri Mahasaya, Sri Yukteswar, and Paramahansa Yogananda.

Our next stop was the Taj Mahal in Agra. Built in the mid-1600s out of white marble, it is one of the Seven Wonders of the Ancient World. Without planning it, we arrived on an evening when the moon would be full—the best possible way to view the Taj. As the Indian sun began to sink below the western horizon, the silvery moon slowly began to rise in the east, casting a mystical otherworldly glow on everything. Lightly dressed for the warm April heat, we hired a rickshaw to take us from our hotel to the Taj. As we approached the entrance, our driver instructed us to turn our heads until he gave the cue to turn around to get the complete view of the Taj, which we hadn't yet seen full on. He soon brought the rickshaw to a halt, gave us the cue, and we both turned around. We immediately became awestruck by the moonlit shimmering white marble mausoleum set in front of us as if in a vision. After spending several hours walking through the various rooms and admiring the inlaid precious and semiprecious stones, and the amazing craftsmanship, we returned to our hotel and had a sumptuous meal to celebrate the experience. We returned the next day, but after our experiences the night before, the second visit was an anticlimax.

Kashmir is considered to be one of the most beautiful travel destinations in the world, and when our plane touched down in Srinagar, we could see why. With its floating gardens and canopied houseboats, it is known as the Venice of the East. Two of its lakes, Dal and Nagin, are jewels surrounded by the majestic Himalayas and flower-filled

meadows. Overwhelmed by the beauty of this mountain paradise, we decided to rent a walnut-wood houseboat on Dal Lake rather than stay in a hotel. Included in the rental were two servants and a great cook. The furnishings inside the boat were all masterfully carved out of walnut, and the window treatments and tables were draped with handmade ivory-colored lace, altogether exuding a feeling of warmth and comfort.

Upon awakening the next day, we opened the wooden shutters covering the windows after a peaceful night's sleep, and were immediately assaulted by what seemed to be about fifty merchants all shouting at the same time, "Please, sir, nutcracker, you buy; oh please, friend, beautiful rug; no, mister, no buy from this crook," and so on and so on. Chris and I couldn't stop laughing. After breakfast we decided to hire a *shikara*, similar to a gondola, to explore the lake with its floating vegetable and flower gardens and awe-inspiring views. We hired the boat and set out on our journey through winding canals with beauty and charm around each corner. Moving into the main channel, we were spotted once again by what seemed to be an armada of merchants rowing quickly toward us and waving their goods in the air. We made it back to our houseboat just in time, climbed aboard, and closed all the shutters. It was like a scene out of an old Abbot and Costello movie! Before leaving Kashmir, we bought some beautiful artifacts to take home as gifts for friends and family.

Indian philosophy teaches that the mere sight of a God-realized master, or taking the dust from their feet, can profoundly change someone if they are receptive. After leaving Kashmir, we returned to our pilgrimage itinerary, visiting Rishikesh on the Ganges and then down to Haridwar—both holy destinations visited regularly by devout Hindus. As good fortune would have it, shortly after our late afternoon arrival and just as the sun was setting over the Ganges, I asked a passerby if Ananda Moyi Ma was at her ashram. I knew she was still

alive, though getting up in years, and that she had an ashram in Harid-war, but somehow doubted she would be there. To my amazement, he nodded yes and kindly escorted Chris and me to the location where she was giving *darshan*, a Sanskrit word denoting the blessings given by a master to his disciples as they approach and prostrate themselves before their guru. We waited in line, and when my turn came, I knelt before her completely awestruck at the experience: I was kneeling before a God-realized Indian saint that my guru had known. I bathed in the waves of love that permeated the room occupied by such an elevated soul. As I looked into her fathomless dark eyes, I intuited that she knew everything about me, that she was delving nonjudgmentally into all my past incarnations, gazing into the very depths of my soul. A feeling of bliss poured into my heart, an experience I will never forget.

By early May, our six-week holiday was coming to a close, and it was also getting unbearably hot. We had routed our tickets to fly from Delhi to London to pay George a visit on the way back to Los Angeles. Before leaving for India, we had dinner at my house with George, and he asked Chris if he could bring back a specially scented oil called *khas* that he liked. We gave it to him when we visited him at Friar Park. The gardens there in mid-May were beautiful, with spring bulbs flowering everywhere and trees filling out in green after a long cold winter. George loved his gardens, and it was very apparent as we strolled through the many different mini-environments he had created there. He gave us his personal tour, showing us new plantings of trees, shrubs, and flow-ers, along with his explanations of why and where things were planted. While at Friar Park, I played Oberheim synth on the track I had co-written with him called "If You Believe," which wound up on the *George Harrison* album.

Our stay at Friar Park was short, since Chris and I were both anx-ious to get back home to our families. George offered to drive us to

the airport, which was quite a hair-raising experience—his version of driving in a Formula One car at the Grand Prix. I thought to myself, "We survived India with its tigers, cobras, and pythons, and now we're ripping down the M4 motorway at a hundred and twenty miles an hour!" Given the speed we were traveling, we were stopped by a policeman, and as George rolled the window down, the officer politely said, "Oh, Mr. Harrison, sorry, on your way then."

Twelve

HEADIN' HOME

had begun writing new songs for my next album during my trip to India. At times we had to hire cars with drivers to take us to places inaccessible by air or train, and that gave me the opportunity to take out my guitar and start composing. Chris would record my ideas on a cassette deck while we were driving to one of our destinations, trying not to concentrate on the cars and trucks passing each other on the two-lane highways. If you dared look at the road ahead of you, you would swear that someone would certainly crash into you head on, but they always swerved back into their lane at the very last minute. Still, I was able to come up with some ideas for future songs during these journeys of terror!

It felt good arriving back in Los Angeles after having been away from my two boys for so long; we had missed each other a lot and they had grown quite a bit since we last saw one another. I had bought a powerboat a few years before that Justin named *Speedy,* and now that Dorian was five and Justin was seven, I felt comfortable taking them on my own as a single dad to Catalina Island for weekends or longer getaways.

Catalina is one of my favorite places on earth. Though it is only twenty-six miles off the coast of L.A., being there you would think you were on an island off the coast of Mexico. It has a dry, desertlike climate, with roaming herds of bison that were left behind from early Westerns filmed there. Wild boar and goats that the Spanish brought over when they first settled the island are plentiful, as are bald eagles, pelicans, and all other sorts of birds. Most important, the water is a crystal-clear deep blue, making it quite easy to spot flying fish, sea otters, dolphins, and whales, along with many other sea creatures roaming above and below the foaming Pacific, with its underwater forests of kelp—a skin diver's paradise. The boys loved it as well, swimming, snorkeling, and camping out with their friends during the warm summers.

My trips to Catalina over the years played a big role in my songwriting, providing me with inspiration and enhancing my relationship with God in nature. As my guru so beautifully expressed,

God the Beautiful is manifest in the synchronized scenery of nature. His breath is heaving in the wind; His divinity is smiling at us in the flowers. The qualities of love and peace and joy that grow in the garden of human hearts are reflecting His goodness, His beauty.[26]

Headin' Home, my fourth album for Warner Bros., was a departure from my last three albums inasmuch as I decided to use guitars once again, the first time since having left Spooky Tooth. After doing some research and calling friends, I decided to use John Haeny as my engineer. John had worked with Jackson Browne, Bonnie Raitt, Linda Ronstadt, and many other great artists. I let him oversee the updating of my studio, which included buying a new Tangent mixing console, an M3 multitrack tape machine and several microphones, compressors, and other outboard gear. It was quite a sonic leap for me—I now had a state-of-the-art studio in my home. I recorded the basic tracks at Davlen

Sound Studios in North Hollywood, and did most of the overdubbing of synths and vocals at my home studio, with the exception of some vocal tracks at Cherokee Studios, where I mixed the album. It was nice to take a more organic approach in producing and recording this album, and I decided to invite some musician friends I'd admired over the years to sing and play on several tracks.

On drums were Alan White, Andy Newmark, Jeff Porcaro, and Harvey Mason; and on percussion Paulinho da Costa, Audie Watkins, Lenny Castro, Emil Richards, and Ralf Humphries. Bobby Lyle played piano and Rhodes on the album, and Jai Winding, Mike Boddicker, and Neil Larsen added their touch on additional synths. Buzzy Feiton, Hugh McCracken, Fred Tackett, Roland Bautista, and Steve Lukather were on guitars; and Jim Horn played a sax solo on "Keep Love in Your Soul." Venetta Fields, Sherlie Matthews, and my sister Lorna Lee sang backing vocals. I had met Steve Lukather through Steve Porcaro during *The Dream Weaver* touring days, before they both went on to be founding members of Toto, along with Steve's brothers Jeff and Mike. Steve Lukather's solos on "Keep Love in Your Soul" and "I Can Feel You Cryin'" were amazing. My friends Graham Nash and David Crosby offered to sing backing vocals with me on "Love's Awake Inside," and one of my all-time favorite singers, Michael McDonald, sang harmony vocals with me on "I'm the One Who'll Be by Your Side." I played Moog bass and the rest of the synth parts as well as piano on "Let Me Feel Your Love Again."

I wrote all of the songs by myself, with the exception of cowriting lyrics on three of the tracks, and I also produced the album alone. John Haeny was a big help in getting great sounds on everything we recorded, as well as doing an excellent job mixing the album. *Headin' Home* still holds up for me, and is still one of my personal-favorite albums. Despite having some of the biggest and best names in the business alongside me on the record, and though it received critical acclaim in-

ternationally, it was not a big hit. Somehow, that was OK with me and I didn't take it personally, as I had on *The Light of Smiles* and *Touch and Gone*. Music was my life, and I knew I would always be involved with it whether with or without big hits. I also wanted to raise my boys, and deciding not to tour was the right move for me. Most important, meditating daily allowed me to keep things in perspective—not getting sucked into the drama of life.

Having more free time and wanting to dive deeper into my spiritual path, I began to make periodic visits to the Mother Center to visit Sri Daya Mata. Ma spent more than twenty years with Yogananda recording all his lectures in shorthand to keep the message of Kriya Yoga alive for future generations. The translation of her name in Sanskrit is "mother of compassion," which she truly was. When George came to L.A. feeling a bit down spiritually, he would often ask me to arrange a meeting with her and we'd drive to Mother Center together. How touching it was to watch him *pranam* and then take the dust off her feet when he first greeted her, as they do in India. In her presence we became like little boys, bathing in the love she exuded. On one such occasion I became so overwhelmed with waves of love permeating the room that I began crying—not from sadness, but from pure joy—one of the most beautiful experiences I'd ever had. That was how we would recharge our spiritual batteries. Problems melted away, as though God was saying, "It's all right now, my child."

On one of my visits to Daya Mata, she suggested I contact the actor Dennis Weaver and his wife, Gerry, who were also devotees. "I think you would get on well together, Gary, as you both share similar careers," she said, seemingly knowing something I wasn't aware of. I found out through a friend that Dennis and Gerry both attended a Tuesday night two-hour meditation at the home of Brenda and John Rosser in Hollywood, so I contacted Brenda and asked if I could come to one of their meditations. I didn't have much experience with long

group meditations and tried to control my inner restlessness as best I could without disturbing anyone. I think I did fairly well for my first time, probably because I was surrounded by seasoned meditators whose collective focus I somehow tuned into. I later found out that it's easier to go deep during long group meditations because there is a united effort of will, making it easier to feel and communicate with God's presence and thus achieve deeper states of consciousness. At the end of the meditation, I introduced myself to Dennis and Gerry, who were warm and gracious; I felt an immediate connection with them, as I did with Brenda and John, who invited me to return as a regular every Tuesday evening. I felt honored by their invitation.

Brenda's father was Dr. Minott W. Lewis, one of Yogananda's first disciples, when he first arrived in Boston in 1920 to begin lecturing and

Gary with Dennis Weaver, circa 1995.
(Photo by Rose Wright.)

building an organization at the behest of his guru back in India, Sri Yukteswar. They met on Christmas Eve and the doctor asked Yogananda if he could explain such passages in the Bible as "If thine eye be single, thy whole body shall be full of light." He had asked many people but was unable to receive a satisfactory answer. The doctor then asked, "Do you think I could see such things?" "I think so," the master replied. He then asked the doctor to sit in front of him on a tigerskin rug that was laid out on the floor, and he began to calm the doctor's restless mind. Placing his forehead against Dr. Lewis's, he instructed him to lift his eyes and look at the point between the eyebrows. The great light of the spiritual eye then appeared with its golden light encircling a dark blue center manifesting the Christ Consciousness—God's presence in creation—and finally a tiny silver star at the very center manifesting Cosmic Consciousness—the highest state of consciousness one can achieve. In this rare experience of Cosmic Consciousness, the awareness is expanded throughout and beyond all creation; breathing ceases and the heart stops beating while in this expanded state.

Only a God-realized master has the ability to transmit this experience to a disciple. A guru doesn't bestow that kind of blessing to everyone; they had obviously been together in previous incarnations and the doctor was very advanced spiritually to have been able to receive the kind of energy that Cosmic Consciousness transmits. That was the beginning of a long relationship, which lasted until Yogananda left his body in 1952; the doctor became vice president of the organization until his passing in the mid-1960s.

I continued attending the group meditations and began to notice the results in my spiritual growth. Both depth of concentration and length of time are necessary to have a successful meditation, and in addition to practicing daily, my guru recommended slowly working up to two to three hours one day a week if I wanted to advance spiritually. I quickly learned that the mind could not control itself without meditation tech-

niques, and that trying to do so simply by sitting in silence was both fruitless and frustrating. Initially what really drew me into his path were the meditation techniques my guru gave, which helped still the restless mind, breath, and heart rate, allowing me to go deep in divine communion and actually feel the presence of God. The *rishis*, sages of ancient India, early on discovered that there was a relationship between the mind, breath, and heart rate, and that if one could still the breath by using a technique of concentration, the heart would then slow down along with the mind. The endless stream of thoughts would settle down, in the way that the distorted image of the moon reflected on a lake settles after a tempest. One then has the experience of real stillness, where the awareness of the soul and God's presence begins to manifest. But this takes time, and patience is a necessity if you want to reach the goal of Cosmic Consciousness.

As expressed by Yogananda,

The more you feel peace in meditation, the closer you are to God. He moves nearer and nearer to you the deeper you enter into meditation. The peace of meditation is the language and embracing comfort of God. Therefore, God is present right on the throne of peace within you. Find Him there first and you will find Him in all the noble pursuits of life, in true friends, in the beauty of nature, in good books, in good thoughts, in noble aspirations. . . . When you know God as peace within, then you will realize Him as peace existing in the universal harmony of all things without.[27]

I now regularly attended the weekly long meditations, and I began to get closer to Dennis and Gerry Weaver, as well as another well-known actor, Jim Arness, who played along with Dennis in the hit TV series *Gunsmoke*. Jim was also a devotee who attended the Tuesday evening meditations at the Rossers'. I never had any other well-known

actor friends, so this was a new experience for me, having the spiritual connection as a common bond between us. Mama Lewis, Dr. Lewis's wife and Brenda's mother, knew Yogananda very well, as he lived with the Lewis family in Boston shortly after arriving in America in 1920. She had some great stories about her guru to share with us when we gathered at their desert retreat in Borrego Springs for the annual eight-hour Christmas meditation that the guru initiated while still in the body. Two hours east of San Diego, the retreat was where Dr. Lewis spent hours in deep meditation, and I felt those vibrations the first time I entered the home. Traditionally, there was always a feast after the meditation, and during those occasions, we would all coax Mama to tell us some of her early recollections with her guru. Feisty and direct, she would call things as they were without beating around the bush. I was mesmerized by the experiences she shared, giving us a glimpse into the depth of who Yogananda was—an avatar, or divine incarnation in the flesh.

One story took place on Plymouth Bay near Dr. Lewis's father's summer home in Duxbury, Massachusetts. His father had a small sailboat he liked to take out for cruises with friends and family members. On one such occasion, a storm came up unexpectedly, and the doctor, his father, and brother were struggling to get back to shore, rowing frantically against the strong winds that were taking them out to sea. Yogananda had once told the doctor that if you are in the Om vibration and your consciousness is centered at the Christ Center in the forehead, nothing can harm you. Remembering these instructions and focusing his attention on the spiritual eye, he began to feel a sense of peace and security. Needless to say, they made it back to shore safely, thankful that the ordeal was over. That evening, when the doctor returned to his home in Somerville, the phone began ringing as he entered the front door. When he answered, it was Yogananda casually remarking, "Well, Doctor, you came near getting wet today, didn't you?" Years later, an-

other devotee, who was with Yogananda at the precise moment of the near-fatal event in Plymouth Bay, said that he suddenly jumped up and threw his book on the floor exclaiming, "The doctor is in trouble, serious trouble." The all-knowing faculty of omniscience was very present in the guru, who always instantly knew if one of his own was at risk. He also had the power to stand between a devotee and his karma, which I personally experienced at the age of sixteen when I was nearly killed in the car crash that killed my two friends.

At Christmastime in the desert, we would always meditate the morning after the eight-hour Saturday meditation, and I remember one occasion where I was transported to a level I'd never before experienced. The hours I put in the day before had prepared me for the depth I was experiencing—such incredible peace. Later that day, I said goodbye to my friends and drove back to L.A. because I was leaving the next morning for Maui, where I was spending Christmas with my family. The peace and love I had experienced the day before was still with me. Whenever I closed my eyes I could feel God's presence ever so near. Over the next few days, as I strolled through the gardens, watched sunsets, or gazed at the floral beauty so present in Hawaii, I could feel Him. Nothing material seemed important anymore in the state of consciousness I was in. It gradually faded away, but the memory has stayed with me to this day.

I still maintained my contact with George even though he was in England and I was in L.A. We usually saw one another several times during any given year, and I continued playing on his albums and writing songs with him such as "If That's What It Takes" from *Cloud Nine*, which we cowrote with Jeff Lynne. I visited his home in Maui several times, where we would spend many hours planting exotic tropical flowers and plants in his garden—a passion we both shared. But what surprised me most was that whenever I asked him the name of a particular plant, he was often able to quickly recite the name to me in Latin.

Perched on a nearby cliff overlooking the Pacific, his home was on several acres of land with beautiful tropical landscaping that showed his touch everywhere. Unlike the U.K., where one had only a few months to plant before the cold winters would set in, Maui was paradise for him as an avid gardener, where one could plant throughout the year.

He loved totally immersing himself in the garden, planting unusual flowers and shrubs bare-handed. Many times he would even take videos of what he'd done so he could observe his work that evening and make corrections the next day. As we planted or pulled weeds together, our conversations would invariably be centered on spirituality and the insights we each had from our own personal experiences. God manifests His presence in the beauty of the cosmos, and the beauty of nature is God reminding us of His presence. He smiles at us in the flowers; we feel His power in the oceans; He stimulates our minds and aspirations in the mountains; and we feel His vast omnipresence and expansiveness in the deserts. I could definitely feel His presence amid that tropical beauty with the vast Pacific in the background. Hawaii and I have some kind of karmic relationship; my son Dorian, who is also a disciple of Yogananda, lives on Oahu and teaches Hatha Yoga and meditation at his studios under the name Power Yoga Hawaii. I'm so pleased because he's totally fulfilled in what he does—certainly one of the chief ingredients of happiness in life.

Thirteen

SOUTH AMERICA

I t was springtime in Los Angeles in 1979, and it seemed like it had been raining for weeks—not a common occurrence in Southern California. I was growing impatient with the dreary weather, while at the same time my strong sense of duty was pushing me to start writing songs for my next album. Somehow I just couldn't get inspired. There was also an urge growing in me to travel somewhere I'd never been before, where I could refocus on the big picture of my life. Who knows, perhaps I might even be inspired to write some songs along the way? I'd always loved the rhythms that came out of South America, especially Brazil. After spending several days mulling this over, I picked up the phone and once again called my friend and travel companion, Chris Agajanian.

"Chris, this weather is getting to me and I think it's time we take another travel break. We had such a great time in India last year. I was thinking of South America this time, with its rain forests and primitive tribes in the Amazon basin, Carnival in Rio, and Machu Picchu in Peru. George told me he'll be at the Grand Prix in São Paulo sometime in February, and we could all meet up there. I could even do some

promotion on my *Headin' Home* album while there. What do you think?" He loved the idea and we both started planning the trip. Because of the vast distances involved in traveling through South America, it made sense to visit only three countries, so we chose to travel to Brazil first, then Argentina, and finally Peru. We would first fly to Manaus, the old rubber capital of Brazil right in the middle of the rain forest on the Rio Negro. After Manaus, we'd fly to Salvador in Bahia, followed by Rio de Janeiro and São Paulo, then on to Buenos Aires in Argentina, and finally end the trip in Peru with a visit to Lima, Cuzco, and Machu Picchu.

A few weeks later, we were on a plane heading for Manaus, with a short stopover in Panama City. When we arrived, we discovered that Chris's bags hadn't made the flight, a major inconvenience. But that was only part of the problem. Since we had decided to book our own hotels to give us more flexibility during the trip, when we checked with the tourist desk at Manaus airport, they informed us that there was a sanitation workers convention in town, and that the entire city was sold out. Our only choice was to stay on a bargelike floating hotel in the middle of the Negro River, where people go at night to view alligators and other wildlife. When I arrived at the front desk, I was greeted by a four-inch-long cockroach scurrying across the check-in counter—another night of roach terror and who knows what else. In addition, we were also told there were only two boats that went into town a day; one in the early morning and another at sundown. After two nights, we collected our bags, checked out, and decided to park ourselves in the lobby of the supposedly best hotel in Manaus, the Tropical. We vowed to stay there until we got rooms, and our tenacity paid off. Not only were we given beautiful accommodations, but Chris got his suitcase as well and the vacation began.

While at the pool the next day, someone came up to me and said,

"There's someone here who says he knows you. He's an English musician." "But who could know me down here?" I thought. I walked over to the restaurant and to my amazement there was Mick Jones. "Now what an uncanny coincidence this is, meeting you in the middle of the rain forest," I blurted out. After exchanging bear hugs, Mick told me he was on a little break and wanted to go somewhere he'd never been, hence Manaus. We spent the next few days as tourists taking short hikes in the nearby jungle, while reminiscing over the years we spent working together before his career with Foreigner exploded into huge success. I was overwhelmed by the different kinds of plants I saw in the rain forest—a kind of world pharmacy waiting to be discovered. Mick and I bid our farewells, and Chris and I prepared for our first adventure: visiting an indigenous tribe of South American Indians, taking me back to my childhood and my fascination with Native Americans. We decided to hire a guide to take us to the rain forest village and escort us back to Manaus. He arranged for the plane, followed by a boat ride into the backwaters of the Amazon, and I had my guitar and cassette player ready should the inspiration strike me in this strange new land on the equator.

We boarded a single-engine plane that would take us as close as possible to where the small houseboat would be waiting for us. I got a little suspicious when I saw people making the sign of the cross as the pilot got into his seat—there was no enclosed cockpit nor fear of hijacking in those days. I keenly observed the pilot trying to start the plane, but nothing seemed to be happening. He finally punched the instrument panel with his fist and the engine started. I became a bit anxious knowing that there were lightning storms every day in the rain forests, and that we were only in a single-engine plane. I closed my eyes and began to meditate, remembering that there was always an eternal connection with God, who was constantly protecting me.

Landing safely, we were transported to our small houseboat to meet the captain and his wife, who only spoke Portuguese. We would all sleep on hammocks, appropriate for the tropics, and after unpacking we immediately set out on a twenty-hour journey on a small river snaking deep into the rain forest. The boat itself was basic—and I mean really basic—but the captain and his wife were very warm and friendly, preparing all the meals and providing us periodically during the day with espresso that was so sweet your hair would nearly stand on end. The constellations in the evening sky were all new to me, as we were in the southern hemisphere, and fireflies were everywhere. Sometimes you couldn't tell the difference between the two except for the movement of the fireflies. The balmy breezes, the tropical birds singing, the frogs chirping, and the monkeys howling while the moon peeked in and out of the partly cloudy sky set a wonderfully mystical mood as we sailed down the gentle river. God's presence as beauty in nature and throughout creation is certainly unparalleled, and you could see that here. There seems to always be a subtle reminder—maybe a feeling or a peaceful undercurrent—that He's right there with you.

Gary Wright, Brazil, circa 1979. *(Photo courtesy of Chris Agajanian.)*

I had bought some percussion instruments before we started our trip, in case there were any jam sessions in store with the locals. During the course of the day, we'd make several stops to buy food that the captain's wife would prepare for us. While we waited for the food to cook, some of the locals would come aboard, and I'd get out my acoustic guitar and we'd all start jamming together. It was so much fun, and it seemed that everyone could play an instrument in their relaxed happy manner. From these impromptu jam sessions, several songs were written or started that wound up on future albums, with the help of Chris in the recording process. After turning along several increasingly smaller tributaries, we finally reached the village, where we were greeted by the tribe. They were very shy and we gave them several bags of sweets, which was like gold to them. They showed us how they hunted with their bows and arrows and blowguns, and took us on a small hike through the surrounding jungle, showing us various plants they used as medicine for treating illness. Unfortunately, given our time constraints, we had to leave fairly soon to continue our journey, so we said our good-byes and started back.

When we arrived at the captain's village, we were told that there was no plane back to Manaus that week due to bad weather, so we had to return by boat on the Amazon. Our guide arranged the details and drove us back in a small boat with no muffler, after telling us stories of giant catfish overturning small boats and dragging the occupants underwater. Then there were of course the thirty-foot-long anacondas, who also were in the river in case someone fell overboard. In the middle of the night, there was a giant crash and the boat felt like it was coming apart. We had struck a sandbar; the captain had to climb out of the boat to free us as well as repair the ropes that had come loose on the impact. I then realized that the boat we were traveling on was more like a Robinson Crusoe raft haphazardly tied together with ropes, and here we were broken down on the Amazon, ready to be dinner for some giant

creature. But we made it back without any more problems, greatly re-
lieved at not having to hear the fully exposed engine with no muffler
that nearly made us all deaf!

Bahia is known for its spicy foods and hospitable people. It is home
to many well-known musicians, Gilberto Gil being one of them. It was
the next stop on our journey, and the local rep for Warner Bros. in Bra-
zil was quite helpful in making introductions, as many of the artists
rarely had the opportunity to meet American musicians. Gilberto gra-
ciously welcomed us into his home and served us some local refresh-
ments, which were spicy, but delicious. We soon started talking about
his music, and he took out his nylon-string guitar and started playing us
some of his songs. What an unusual voice and style of singing and play-
ing he had—we were enraptured by his songs and didn't want him to
stop our private concert. Soon, another friend and fellow well-known
artist dropped by, Baby Consuelo. She started singing and Chris and I
were blown away by her beautiful voice. What was refreshing about
that experience was that neither had any agendas to lay on us; we were
embraced by their warmth and made to feel totally at home. Years later,
from 2003 to 2008, Gilberto served as Brazil's minister of culture in
the administration of President Luiz Inácio Lula da Silva.

Leaving Bahia and flying south toward Rio, I looked down at the
mouth of the Amazon flowing into the South Atlantic in what seemed
to be hundreds of miles of brown river water mixing with the ocean—
an amazing spectacle of nature's raw power. As we landed in Rio,
preparations for Carnival were everywhere and anticipation was build-
ing to an emotional fever-pitch. When the day arrived, the streets were
so jammed with people dressed in everything from simple to outra-
geous costumes, that we decided to watch the spectacle from our hotel
rooms, which were above the parade on the main street. And then it
began: music, dancing, singing, floats all moving along in an endless
procession. There were at least two blocks of tambourine players, an-

other several blocks of snare drums, then bass drums, then shakers, maracas, you name it—it was all there—a cacophony of intermingled sound that was both electrifying and impossible to verbalize. We went to several parties that evening and met some wonderful people through the Warner rep there. He also arranged for me to go into a studio in Rio to record some of the great local percussion players that I could take back to L.A. with me for possible future albums. I went into the studio with the musicians and my acoustic guitar, and started singing some song ideas I had. They played along with me, and then I just let them do their own thing and jam together. I kept the recordings in my studio for years until the right project came along for me to use the tracks.

Next on the agenda was the Grand Prix in São Paulo, where we were to meet George and watch the race the next day. Shortly after landing, we drove to Interlagos, where the race was to take place. The plan was that we were to meet in Emerson Fittipaldi's motor coach after we arrived; Emerson was a good friend of George's and one of the Formula One drivers in the race the next day. George warmly greeted us and immediately introduced us to Emerson; the conversation turned to the upcoming race. Chris, who knew a lot about Formula One racing, asked George if by chance he knew the drivers' names and starting grid positions. George took out a piece of paper and, from memory, wrote them all down for Chris. I was very impressed at both his memory and his knowledge of racing. We soon left for our hotel, where we met another driver and friend of George's—Jackie Stewart. After settling into our rooms, we headed for a restaurant while being chased by the paparazzi and Beatles fans. George was surprisingly calm through it all.

The next morning we were picked up by a helicopter and flown to the track, where we viewed the race from the garage pit area. The actor Gene Hackman was also hanging out there; Chris had known him from the times he attended races at Ascot Raceway. Jacques Laffite, driving a Ligier-Ford, won the race that day.

From left: Chris Agajanian, Gene Hackman, George Harrison, and Gary Wright.

After saying our goodbyes to George, we took off the next day for Buenos Aires. The local Warner Bros. rep was very helpful, arranging interviews and TV shows to promote my *Headin' Home* album, which had just been released there. One of the TV shows I did was in a club on the second story of an older building. In the middle of summer, with no air-conditioning, the room became unbearably hot and we had to open the windows. The DJ interviewing me had an afro, and when they turned the lights up to begin filming, hundreds of flying insects flew in through the windows, right into the DJ's afro. It was so bizarre doing an interview in broken English while this man's head was literally vibrating with trapped bugs—an experience I hope I'll never have to repeat. God loves to play tricks with me sometimes—he has a sense of humor, too.

The following day we were at a café overlooking a quaint square with the Warner rep, and a friendly-looking couple stopped to say hello to our host. Apparently they were old friends, but knew very little English, so we conversed in Spanish. He told them I was an artist from the

States and they graciously asked me for my phone number in case they came to L.A. and needed help. I gave it to them and they did call when they passed through, each time a little more famous in their careers. The couple, Diego Verdaguer and Amanda Miguel, asked me to write some songs with them, which I did. I even wound up coproducing several tracks with them for one of Amanda's albums. They eventually became icons in the Latino music world.

They've become very close friends and we often go on holidays together. Recently, I celebrated my seventieth birthday and was hoping to see Diego and Amanda. They couldn't be there, however, because of their touring schedule. I forgot all about it, and on the night of the event we had a great jazz trio playing music in our home where the party was held. The vibe was great and people were having a good time when all of a sudden a mariachi band burst into my living room while the jazz trio was still playing. I ran up to the leader of the band and shouted, "Hey, you've got the wrong house. I didn't order a mariachi band." They kept on advancing like a giant snake into my living room, when suddenly at the very end of the line of musicians, there were Diego and Amanda, smiling. What a great surprise! He had orchestrated the whole thing, and to make things even better, Diego, who has a great voice, sang some beautiful songs accompanied by the band. That was their birthday present to me and I'll never forget it.

Our final stop was Peru. We spent the first few days in Lima organizing the rest of our itinerary. First, we were to take the train to Cuzco, the ancient center of the Inca Empire that the conquistador Francisco Pizarro vanquished in 1533. The elevation of the city is at nearly eleven thousand feet, and we had to take it easy the first few days. The overall vibe of Cuzco was very friendly, and most of the locals were either Inca or of Inca decent. The Spanish Colonial buildings were picturesque, and the altars in the churches were adorned with pure gold from the days of the Spanish empire. There was even a kind of mystical feeling

one had being there, especially when looking at the millions of stars in the southern hemisphere sky on a clear warm evening. I also distinctly remember having an unusually spiced delicious vegetarian meal at the local Krishna temple restaurant. After a few days in Cuzco, we departed by train to Machu Picchu, the enchanting ancient city perched a thousand feet above the Urubamba River. Known as "the lost city of the Incas," it wasn't discovered until 1911. The views from the ruins of the surrounding valleys were absolutely breathtaking, and while walking through them the day after we arrived, I became inspired to record a video of me singing one of the songs from my *Headin' Home* album, "I'm the One Who'll Be by Your Side." Chris organized and filmed it for posterity. Returning back to Lima, I was beginning to get homesick for my family. We departed the next day for Los Angeles after almost six weeks away from home.

STRUGGLE, GROWTH, AND THEN THE LIGHT

t was late March and it felt great getting back home and settling back in with my two boys. They had missed me and I had missed them—I was usually never away for so long. Chris and I had bought a larger boat, together with a friend of his, Larry Best, a few months before we left for South America. I spent a lot of time that summer at Catalina Island on our new boat, and the boys brought their friends and had regular campouts. Taking their sleeping bags to shore in the dingy, and hoping not to wake up in the middle of a bison herd—which actually happened once when I was with them—they had great times together. The boat was named *C. Dream* and it had a fly bridge, a kitchen, and could sleep up to six people—perfect for our needs.

I began receiving calls from the A&R department at Warner Bros. to discuss recording my new album, and I finally met with Lenny Waronker and Russ Titelman. They suggested I take a fresh look at my career and get another musician involved to coproduce the next album with me. I was internally resistant to the idea at first, but then decided it might be the right move at that time in my career. After several meetings and tossing around several possible choices that didn't quite feel

right, the name Dean Parks came up. I knew him as a great guitar player and musician, and thought he could also help me in arranging the songs on the album. Intuitively I felt he was the right choice, and Lenny and Russ agreed. They phoned Dean and he agreed to work on the project.

I spent a lot of time writing and cowriting the songs for the album, and Dean and I were very picky in choosing the ones we thought would fit best. In addition to Dean's guitar work, Marty Walsh played rhythm guitar on two tracks; Tris Imboden, James Gadson, Bob C. Benberg, and David Kemper were on drums; Lenny Castro on percussion; George Hawkins on bass for one track; and Rod Piazza on harmonica. Timothy B. Schmit, David Pack, my sister Lorna, and I did all the backing vocals.

The album was named *The Right Place* and was released in 1981. I was still using a lot of synthesizers on the album, and played synth bass on all but one track. Dean played the lead synth line on the track "Really Wanna Know You," which became one of the distinguishing "hooks" of the song. We recorded the album in both our studios, and Jay Lewis, the engineer who recorded and mixed *The Dream Weaver* and *The Light of Smiles* albums, mixed it at Hollywood Sound studios. The first single Warner Bros. released was "Really Wanna Know You," a song I'd written with Ali Thomson who had a hit with his song "Take a Little Rhythm" in the late 1970s. When *The Right Place* was first released, radio responded quite favorably to "Really Wanna Know You" and it began climbing the *Billboard* charts. It felt good being in the charts again with a Top 20 hit single, but then a strange sequence of events happened, and it peaked at number 16. It probably would have gone Top 10 or even Top 5, but the week it reached its highest position, the head of radio promotion at Warner Bros. was fired and the track lost all its momentum on the radio. The situation would be analogous to changing quarterbacks in football when you're behind by a touchdown

and are on the five-yard line of your opponent and not scoring. But these are the things over which artists have no control and which make the business so frustrating. The music business was already heading south with the rise of disco, and music videos would change the entire landscape of how record labels would operate in the future.

On another more positive note, I had always felt that the song "Comin' Apart," another one of the tracks on the album, would be a hit. I cowrote it with two of my favorite songwriters, the renowned husband and wife team of Barry Mann and Cynthia Weil—and about twenty-five years later it hit the charts, an aspect of songwriting that I love. You never know who's going to cover one of your songs—especially an obscure one—till you get a publishing royalty statement or a phone call from the publisher. In this case, a well-known DJ named Armand Van Helden took my track, sped it up, added his drum loops, and produced a great dance rendition he retitled, "My My My," which sold over eight million copies internationally—God's cosmic plan working again under His schedule.

The intricacies of the Master Novelist never cease to amaze me. I'll never forget how moved I felt the first time I heard The Righteous Brothers on AM radio in New York singing Barry and Cynthia's "You've Lost That Lovin' Feelin'." But the karmic pathways attracting us to whom we'll meet during a lifetime are extremely subtle, and I never dreamed that one day I would be writing and becoming friends with Barry and Cynthia.

Shortly before I began recording *The Right Place*, Dee and I had decided to go our own ways. It didn't make sense to have a manager anymore since I had stopped touring in order to raise my boys. We still maintained a friendly relationship with each other, but I was concerned about how Warner Bros. would react to my not having a manager and I was beginning to sense that something negative was brewing—especially since the music business was changing so rapidly. My friend

Chris graciously offered to step in as an interim manager, almost daily meeting with Warner Bros. during the promotion of *The Right Place*. But unfortunately it didn't change things. There are times in one's life when trials seem to be flying at you from all directions at the same time, and with the same intensity. This was one of them. Getting over the shock of the sequence of events that led to the poor performance of my last album, *The Right Place*, was extremely difficult for me. I tried to remain positive in spite of what was happening around me. Then I got the painful phone call from Lenny Waronker at Warner Bros. saying that they were dropping me from their label due to weak sales from *The Right Place*. I couldn't believe my ears when I got the news. This, along with the stress from my failed relationship with Christina, was perhaps the most difficult time in my life. I tried to keep my guru's words circulating through my thoughts:

> Since you are made in God's image, to believe that your tests are more difficult than your divinity is powerful to overcome them is to believe in an untruth. Remember, no matter what your tests are, you are not too weak to fight. God will not suffer you to be tempted more than you are able to bear.[28]

I kept meditating daily and moved on from point to point, gradually building myself up again. But spiritual progress is very subtle and moves slowly—even imperceptibly. Still, I had been regular in my meditations, never missing a day; I was even starting to be able to meditate fear and anxiety out of my life for short periods of time. One feels a great sense of power when one can shift attention from God's dualistic drama within creation (maya) to the soul's consciousness of strength, faith in God's protection and omnipotence and fearlessness. All great achievements require sustained effort, and I began to feel I was getting there slowly. The wonderful thing about following the path of yoga is

that it works like mathematics if you practice regularly in meditating, serving and helping others, and watching your thoughts.

When you're severely tested in life, there's usually a reward that comes along, even though you may not immediately recognize it. After my protracted divorce, I wanted to find someone who shared my values and spiritual philosophy. I prayed deeply to God to send me a soul mate to share my life with. My sister Beverly had invited me to a party at a friend's home in Beverly Hills and I brought a date with me, who accidently spilled a cup of coffee on another guest's dress. I profusely apologized and started to help her clean up while my date wandered off, embarrassed by what she'd done. Then out of the blue, I felt prompted to ask her if she knew any single attractive women who had good values and liked kids and raising a family. Surprisingly she didn't think I was weird being so direct with her. She thought for a moment then smiled and told me she knew the perfect person. She gave me a name and a work phone number, which I called a few days later. I think my future partner was put off at first that someone had given out her phone number, but out of curiosity, she agreed to meet me. On November 8, 1983, I met Rose Anthony on a blind date at Café Figaro on Melrose in West Hollywood.

It was a nice low-key first meeting, and we talked about our likes and dislikes, long-term goals, and how we spent our leisure time. Rose lived in Woodland Hills, a part of the San Fernando Valley, and at the time was the administrative assistant to the owner of Apple One employment agency, Bernie Howroyd. The company became one of the largest independently owned employment agencies in the country. Bernie was a great role model for her, always positive and supportive of his employees. When she asked me about my career, I told her I was a songwriter and she just smiled. I didn't want to tell her that I was a celebrity for fear of putting her off. She had never been married before, but loved family. A few dates later, I opened my life up to her, telling

her about who I was, my divorce, and having joint custody of two boys, to see if she still wanted to see me. None of this fazed her.

We slowly began to build a relationship, and in time, fell in love with each other. For me it was a dream come true being in a relationship with someone who was nurturing, understanding, and so supportive of me and my work. I felt like I was starting out again, only this time with someone deeply committed to me. Coming from a family with eight children, she loved kids and provided a wonderful support for me, helping and encouraging me to rebuild my life. She became the rock of our family. One memory I will always cherish was when we were in my garden on a November Saturday afternoon, and I mentioned to her that I was thinking of selling my boat. "You don't sell a boat, you get a bigger one," she answered with a smile. Her dad, who had worked for Bob Hope, owned a 55-foot cabin cruiser, so she grew up around boats and knew a lot about them. A great cook as well, she prepared some wonderful meals on the boat while we vacationed at

Rose

Catalina Island. Anchoring in a tranquil harbor; I stretched out in my hammock while reading inspiring books or writing songs.

A few weeks into our relationship, I took her to the Lake Shrine, and I could see that she immediately felt at home being there. Like me, she was raised Catholic, and had attended Catholic school. As a senior in high school, she took a world religion course, visiting the Vedanta Society in Hollywood, and immediately felt attuned with the vibration there. She made several return visits and became very interested in Eastern philosophy. Being at the Lake Shrine seemed to rekindle those feelings in her. I bought her a copy of *Autobiography of a Yogi*, and she told me she felt like she was coming home while reading it. Unbeknownst to me, she subscribed to the lessons and began to meditate and learn the techniques. It touched me very deeply that without any prompting from me, she became a disciple, deepening our relationship further. We married in October 1985 at the Lake Shrine temple, where on that magical evening ten years earlier, I first attended the lecture given by the monk from SRF. Shortly before getting married, Rose received initiation into Kriya Yoga. All the beautiful elements seemed now to be falling into place. Exchanging Yogananda's wedding vows was a very emotional moment for both of us. As we walked down the aisle at the end of the ceremony, to my great surprise, there was George in the last row dressed in white and smiling. Earlier I had told him we were getting married but didn't give him any details, as I thought he'd be in the U.K. I think he found out the details through his sister-in-law Linda Arias, who was also a devotee and close friend of Rose and me. He drove my two boys Justin and Dorian back to our home where the reception was being held, probably at ninety miles an hour. A big Formula One fan, he still loved racing and fast cars. I'm sure the boys didn't mind. Rose and I left the next day for our honeymoon in India.

I knew we must be someplace exotic as our taxi driver drove us to our hotel in Singapore and we passed a large billboard with a sign

reading, "It's now Shanghai hairy crab season." "My taste buds are about to go on a new adventure," I mused. We spent the first day of our honeymoon sightseeing and got caught in an equatorial downpour while walking through a tropical botanical garden in one of the parks. With the time difference being fifteen hours ahead of Los Angeles and since we were leaving the next morning for Madras, we had an early night.

I'd never been to southern India before, and my first impression after we landed was that it was distinctly different from the north in its languages, food, and style of temples. You know you're back in India when you're in a cab and want to open the window but there's no window opener. The taxi driver sees your dilemma, stops the car, jumps out, and pulls a car window opener out of his pocket and opens your window. It was great being back!

Our plan was to have an Indian wedding at our guru's ashram in Ranchi, which is in the north, and we had made arrangements in L.A. for one of the SRF ministers, Brother Bimalananda, a direct disciple of Yogananda—to marry us, as he would also be in India when we .vere there. While in Madras, we met up with Kamala Chakravarti, Lakshmi Shankar's sister, whom I'd met on my first trip to India with George. Kamala helped Rose pick out a wedding sari as well as some jewelry; she also took us on a tour of some south Indian temples. Rose and I were beginning to feel that beautiful devotion for God that's always present in India. We also felt that our guru was guiding us and managing all the details of our trip perfectly—a beautiful wedding present. We had decided back in L.A. to spend some time at a beach resort, and found the perfect place—Mahabalipuram—right on the Indian Ocean. Our ocean-front room was perfect, and every night we had a feast at the hotel. Now, southern Indian food can be very spicy, and I made the mistake of ordering something "spicy"—after the first bite I thought my hair would stand on end. Really! I learned that lesson quickly. We had

peaceful, long romantic walks on the beach and sometimes would even watch the hotel's female gardening staff cut the grass with small hand sickles.

After our few days in the south, we flew to Ranchi to organize and prepare for our Indian wedding. We had to fly to Calcutta, stay overnight, and then leave the next day for our final destination. Our flight to Ranchi was in a twin-engine prop plane, and just before we took off, the hostesses served the food. People starting eating even as passengers were still boarding, and I noticed one heavy-set gentleman was having difficulty getting into his seat. He started pushing down the seat in front of him, which was occupied, and actually pushed the person's face into his vegetarian lunch. The poor man got up and started screaming at the perpetrator, but the damage had been already done. It was like a scene out of a slapstick comedy. About an hour into the trip, I looked out the window and noticed black oil streaming out of one of the engines. I thought to myself, "I'm on my honeymoon and we're going to crash in the tiger-infested Bengali jungle." Since almost everyone on the plane was Hindu and believed in reincarnation, there was no fuss at all. But we had to turn around and fly back to Calcutta because Ranchi didn't have the parts to repair the plane. We landed smoothly, followed by the fire brigade armed with pails of sand in case of fire. We took the next plane out and arrived safely in Ranchi.

Upon our arrival at the ashram, the monk who was to marry us asked if we would mind if he invited some of the Indian devotees who had never heard Yogananda's wedding vows. We agreed and word spread like wildfire, since we were there during their annual week of lectures, meditations, and Kriya Yoga initiations called *Sharad Sangam*. Weddings in Indian culture sometimes last a week and are a big event in one's life. According to custom, which varies regionally, the families dress and prepare the bride and groom. A wonderful family from Gujarat, the Divalkas, offered to dress and prepare both of us. Rose's hands

and feet were painted in artistic patterns with henna, and her sari was assembled in the Gujarati style. When women saw her makeup bag, they laughed and took out their charcoal pencils and did her makeup; they also helped Rose with her jewelry.

I wore a turban and traditional wedding pajamas, again in Gujarati style, and had a strand of pikake flowers attached to my turban, which hit me in the nose every time I turned my head. As is the custom, I also carried a coconut with several rupees as a material offering. When we both arrived in the packed temple where the service was being held, the monk doing the ceremony took one look at us and started laughing— he'd never seen us in such regalia. "God's having some fun today," I thought. In the Hindu fashion, we walked around the ceremonial fire while reciting the beautiful wedding vows written by our guru while our fellow devotees watched. The memory of the ceremony will always remain in my heart: I had found my soul mate at last.

As a wedding present, Anne Marie Bennstrom, from the Rossers' meditation group, had given Rose and me use of her houseboat on Nagin Lake in Kashmir, which is a well-known Indian honeymoon destination. We arrived there the day after our wedding and were escorted by her local friends to our new floating home. Hand-carved and beautifully furnished, it was the perfect place to relax after the wedding. It was the second week of November high up in the Himalayas, and at night it got very cold. We must have had at least six hot water bottles under our blankets and sheets to warm our bed before retiring at night, and in the early morning, someone would arrive to light our pot-bellied stove so we could sprint to the dresser and put on some warm clothes. Khalik, Anne Marie's friend who looked after her guests, proved to be a wonderful host. He supervised the delicious food we ate on the boat, and even invited us to a Muslim wedding. After a week, it was time to depart for our next destination, Banaras.

Rose was deeply moved to see the Ganges for the first time, as well

as the ancestral home of Lahiri Mahasaya. I found out that Ravi Shankar was in Banaras, and when I called him, he invited us to his home. As we arrived, he was giving music lessons to his pupils while at the same time being filmed. There was also a French artist in the room sculpting a bust of his head. Rose felt a bit overwhelmed as she entered the room, but Ravi graciously embraced us and invited us to a delicious vegetarian lunch, which we ate on banana leaves while sitting cross-legged on the floor—not one of my favorite eating positions. Ravi picked this up and had several pillows brought in. After lunch, we said our goodbyes and left the following day for a short trip to the Taj Mahal, followed by a visit to the holy city of Brindaban, or Vrindaban, as it is called today.

Considered one of the holiest places in India and comparable to Jerusalem in the Christian religion, Brindaban is where Lord Krishna played out the drama of his life as a divine avatar, just as Jesus did in Jerusalem. Loved by millions of Hindus who make yearly pilgrimages to this holiest of holy areas of India, His presence can be felt everywhere. After a brief rest in our hotel after arriving, Rose and I went for a walk along the banks of the sacred Yamuna River, where as a cowherd in his youth, Krishna played his flute, entertaining the local milkmaids and his consort, Radha. The Indian sun was beginning to set and a gentle breeze caressed us as we sat and watched the river flow by. I felt that Krishna was there with us.

I slept very deeply that night and woke up early the next morning to chanting coming from the nearby temples, a beautiful way to greet the day. We had a car drive us to Mathura, the birthplace of Lord Krishna, and after visiting several temples, we walked to the Keshav Dev Temple, which was built in ancient times on the site of His birthplace. As the story is told, He was actually born in an underground prison. Following the custom when visiting holy places in India, we left our shoes outside the entrance and walked down a long tunnel to the site of the

birthplace. As I was barefoot, I could feel the stone floor of the tunnel, which was worn smooth by the millions of truth seekers who visited this sacred place daily over perhaps thousands of years. The vibrations of devotion seemed to permeate everything around us as we stood and prostrated ourselves before the deity—a symbol of the Lord himself. It seemed like time stood still as Rose and I became absorbed in the beauty of the moment. After a vegetarian lunch, we returned to our hotel and slowly let the day wind down. I reflected on George telling me a secret desire he had of spending the later years of his life roaming the banks of the Ganges or Yamuna rivers with the yogis and sadhus, being lost in God.

Fifteen

WHO I AM

Our honeymoon came to a close and we flew back to Los Angeles to prepare for Thanksgiving, which we always have with friends and family at our home. Rose has a gift for making our guests feel at home while she serves culinary masterpieces in our candlelit dining room in front of a roaring fire. The Christmas season shortly followed, which included our traditional eight-hour meditation, shifting our focus to the spirit of giving and feeling the presence of Christ everywhere. I greeted the New Year with the resolution to write more songs as well as score more films. As early as 1982, I had begun to turn my attention to scoring movies again after having composed the music for my first film, Willy Bogner's *Benjamin*, while still living in England in the early seventies. In 1982, after leaving Warner Bros. Records, I composed the music score to Alan Rudolph's *Endangered Species*, starring Robert Urich and JoBeth Williams. The film was critically acclaimed and I enjoyed working with Alan, who gave me great creative latitude during the scoring process.

Later on that year, I received a call from Paramount Pictures, which wanted to set up a meeting with myself, John Travolta, and Sylvester

Stallone. I was extremely curious about why they wanted to meet with me, as I had never met either of them before, and was only aware of their huge careers. When I arrived on the Paramount lot in Hollywood, I was escorted into one of the executive offices where both Sly and John were waiting for me. They warmly greeted me—disarming my nervousness—and Sly explained that Paramount was doing a sequel to *Saturday Night Fever* called *Stayin' Alive*. John would play the leading role and Sly would direct. They wanted me to do the music—which of course I was thrilled to hear—and after a few weeks of working out contractual issues, I was ready to begin. Quite honestly, I was really excited to be part of a project that had such star power; working with a major studio like Paramount would be a huge bonus to my career. I began sending Sly music for the various scenes he sent to me requiring score. Things were going along very well until I noticed that Sly's brother Frank also began providing music for some of the same scenes I had already done. Given that Sly was directing, I feared that Frank's music might wind up replacing a lot of my work. When the film was completed, I went to a screening that confirmed my hunch. A lot of my music was in the film, but not to the degree I was led to believe from my initial meetings. Such are the fortunes of Hollywood.

Shortly after Rose and I married, Willy Bogner contacted me about working on a new project he was directing called *Fire and Ice*. The film was an extravaganza of his trademark spectacular cinematography, featuring top stunt figures John Eaves and Suzy Chaffee performing their skills on majestic snowcapped mountain ranges in both Europe and North America. It won the Bavarian Film Award in Germany in 1987, for best single artistic achievement. The songs and music score were provided by me, Harold Faltermeyer, Alan Parsons, and John Denver, and the soundtrack got into the Top 10 in the German music charts. Several of my songs were also on a later release of Willy's called *Ski to the Max*, which featured some of P!nk's music as well. I've been blessed

in this lifetime to have been surrounded by very creative people—Willy being one of them. The chemistry of his images have created a perfect match for my music. Not only a director, Willy owns a line of very chic, well-made clothing, which includes high-end ski and sportswear conceived by cutting-edge designers. His Brazilian wife, Sônia, has her own exclusive designer collection called Sônia Bogner.

Gary en route to meet with Willy Bogner in Germany, circa 1990.
(Photo by Rose Wright.)

We've spent some great holidays together, and on one occasion on St. Croix in the Caribbean, we did a photo shoot. (One of the photos was eventually used for the cover of my album *First Signs of Life.*) On his sixtieth birthday, which was held in a restaurant on the top of the Piz Corvatsch mountain in St. Moritz, Switzerland, I sang a song I'd written about friendship to honor our long relationship. The lyric in the chorus of the song defined the moment:

A friend like you is like a star that lights my way.
When I feel lost or alone I know there's a home in a friend like you.

When I think of all the gifts God's given me, what greater thing
 could He do?
He gave me a treasure in a friend like you.

Outside it was freezing cold; it had snowed the night before. The sky
appeared to be filled with millions of stars that night, when from be-
hind one of the peaks, shyly and slowly the moon appeared, adding a
glistening light to the white, fresh-fallen snow: a precious moment fro-
zen in time.

It had been a while since I had released an album, and the creative
part of me was beginning to stir. Part of being an artist is the need to
play live—which I had stopped doing in the late seventies—or to be
making an album in the studio. Not fulfilling either of these urges, I
was feeling the need to record again—an album that became *Who I Am*.

I started writing songs and recording them at my home studio,
working with different songwriters, musicians, and arrangers like Steve
Farris, the guitarist from Mr. Mister; Steve Porcaro from Toto; lyricist
John Lang from Mr. Mister; Bruce Gaitsch; and Tom Keane, who
worked with David Foster. Tom's brother John Keane, a drummer
friend of mine, introduced me to Wyn Davis, who owned a great re-
cording studio very near to my home called Total Access. He had an
impressive collection of vintage studio equipment, along with a large
studio where drums and other amplified instruments could be recorded.
We decided to work together on my next project, which he would co-
produce with me.

One afternoon while I was writing in my studio, Teddy Cohen, a
friend of mine from Warner Bros., called me out of the blue to let me
know that he was now working for a new record label called Cypress
Records. My former label, A&M Records, was their distributor, and
they were looking for artists to sign. I had several meetings with Teddy
and Craig Sussman, who owned the label, and decided to do a deal with

them. They owned their own Sony digital multitrack tape machine, which was cutting edge at the time, and we used it to record *Who I Am*. When the songwriting and arranging were finished, I began to assemble the musicians I wanted to play on the album. In the past I had played a lot of the instruments myself, but this time I wanted to do something different; I wanted to put together a group of world-class musicians and record an album with musical influences I'd taken in from my world travels. The emphasis would be on music from India—a newly discovered passion I wanted to explore.

Steve Farris was an invaluable source for great musicians, like keyboardist Alan Pasqua, and bass guitar players Jimmy Haslip from the Yellowjackets and Jimmy Johnson. Wyn recommended drummer Terry Bozzio, and guitarist Michael Thompson—who played some great solos on the album. South Indian classical violinist L. Subramaniam played Indian violin on several tracks, as well as arranging and conducting the south Indian percussion players he chose to use on the project. They were touring in Switzerland at the time and had some days off, so it made more sense for us to fly there and work in a local studio rather than bringing them to L.A. An old Swiss friend of mine, Art Zuber, helped me find a suitable facility to do the recording.

The percussionists spoke little or no English, so everything was filtered through Subramaniam. Powerplay Studios, where we were recording, had a spacious recreation room where we would go to relax during breaks. It had a large pool table, which I don't think the Indians had ever seen before, much less played on. One of the musicians claimed to be an expert pool player, but I noticed that he would make up the rules as the games progressed in a way that always benefited him. Consequently, he would always win while the others stood by looking bewildered and confused—especially after one of them had just sunk two or three balls in a row.

All the Indian players were strict vegetarians; they even brought all

their spices from India and humbly showed our Swiss cook how to use them. I noticed one of the musicians was constantly writing on a small notepad throughout the day and evening when we weren't recording. When I asked Subramaniam what he was writing, he told me, "He's writing down one of the names of God so that his thoughts would constantly be on the Lord"—*japa yoga*. "What a beautiful demonstration of love for God," I thought. There's a saying in the Hindu scriptures: "In shallow men, the fish of little thoughts cause much commotion. In oceanic minds, the whales of inspiration make hardly a ruffle."[29] One of the last items we had to complete was recording Lakshmi Shankar— Ravi Shankar's sister-in-law, an outstanding classical Indian singer who sang a haunting vocal on both "Sad Eyes" and "Voices." It was a very touching moment when Lakshmi walked up to the microphone to begin recording. Wyn had never recorded an Indian vocalist before, and when she began singing, he was deeply touched by the beauty of her voice and his eyes filled with tears. Her voice awakened feelings I don't think we had ever experienced before, and the two tracks she sang on were transported to another level.

We wound up with great performances from our Indian friends and headed back home, excited by what we had accomplished. George was in town at the time and offered to play a slide guitar solo on one of the tracks, "(I Don't Wanna) Hold Back," which added his signature texture to the song. I finished my lead and backing vocals, and we were ready to mix. I was more than pleased with the end result, far beyond my initial expectations of making a "world music" album. I had grown tired of making pop/rock albums and needed this profound change. In retrospect, it's one of my two personal favorite albums and stands the test of time even though it wasn't hugely commercially successful. Wyn did a brilliant job recording and mixing the album, and it was well received critically, especially in Europe.

Shortly before I started recording *Who I Am*, George asked me to host a small dinner party at my home in Los Angeles with Jeff Lynne, whom George was thinking of working with on his new album, *Cloud Nine*. Before Jeff arrived, George sent Rose to the store to buy the ingredients he needed to cook a special Indian meal that night. While she was gone, he asked my boys to set the table. He left the dining room for a short while and upon returning to inspect what the boys had done, he laughed and had them start from scratch, only this time under his supervision, setting a proper English table. The evening went very well and George, Jeff, and I eventually wound up inside my studio, where we had an extended jam session. I could tell that George was enjoying himself and that the chemistry was working between him and Jeff. Several months later we all met again in George's studio at Friar Park in the U.K., where Jim Keltner, Ringo, Jeff, George, and I were to be the rhythm section for *Cloud Nine*. Jeff wound up coproducing the album with George. It was great seeing the two work together. I had always been a big fan of his former band ELO (Electric Light Orchestra); watching his production ideas unfold in the studio was an inspiration.

I was a regular jogger and especially loved jogging in the mornings. Running down the picturesque pathways of Friar Park and passing through the different tastefully landscaped environments my gardening friend had created, I couldn't help but think of God's creative hand working His magic and beauty through George. One morning, to my surprise, George asked if he could join me on my run; I think he wanted to gear up and get in shape before we started to record the album. While jogging, he casually mentioned to me that he wanted to do a remake of an old song, and off the top of my head I said "What about 'I've Got My Mind Set on You,' the old R&B song that was the B-side of the single, 'If You Gotta Make a Fool of Somebody' by James Ray." George was extremely curious about my knowing the song, as he immediately

remembered it as well. I explained to him that I was a big fan of early R&B, and that my first musical influences came from the 1950s and early 1960s, beginning with doo wop.

We started the *Cloud Nine* recording with the songs George had already written, including a song I had cowritten with him and Jeff called "That's What It Takes." One early afternoon, a few weeks after starting the album, we were all together in the studio when Jim Keltner started playing a cool rhythm pattern on his drum machine. An inspiration suddenly came over me and I started singing the chorus to "I've Got My Mind Set on You" while playing a bass line with my left hand and a brass part with my right. George smiled at me while everyone picked up their instruments and we all started playing the chorus. The track came together literally in a matter of minutes. Later on, when the album was released, "Got My Mind Set on You" came out as the first single and went straight to number 1 in the *Billboard* charts. I was so happy for George that he was back at the top again, and I particularly loved the video he made for "Set on You"—especially the part when the George look-alike stuntman did the backflip during the solo section of the song. It had George's humor written all over it!

Another time while we were still recording *Cloud Nine*, his staff had left for the day and the doorbell began ringing continually by someone trying to deliver coal for the fireplaces in the house. George eventually went downstairs to show them where to put the coal, and then came back to the studio to resume playing, when the doorbell rang again. This time, the workers wanted to know where they should leave the bill. Again he had to leave, and when he returned he looked really flustered and said, "I'm only trying to be the guitar player here, but I have to be the butler as well, answering the door and trying to make a hit single at the same time." Rather than becoming angry, he turned the situation into a Monty Python–like skit where the creative person is constantly being bothered by workers. The sketch they did was Beetho-

ven trying to write his Fifth Symphony. Right before he was ready to play the final note, a mynah bird would start loudly screeching or his wife would continuously interrupt him with ridiculous requests. As Beethoven became deafer, he wrote away, oblivious to the racket around him. A great lover of Monty Python, George would create similar skits like this frequently, but sometimes he would also hiss to show he didn't like the bothersome intrusions.

After doing a short promotional tour of Europe to support the release of *Who I Am*, Rose and I returned home and quickly got back into our family routine with the boys, who were now teenagers and very much into music. Justin, the older brother, was into rock music, and Dorian was into R&B. They both were good singers and were even beginning to write songs. While they wanted to pursue careers in music, I advised them to think seriously about it before diving in. I explained to them that the ups and downs and the emotional toll of being an artist could be devastating. "You need to be tough, tenacious, and ready to rebound after any failure," I explained to them. Ultimately, I realized that despite my advice, they had to live their own lives, which they have.

Rose and I had begun to hang out more with Dennis and Gerry Weaver at their new house in Malibu. Brenda and John Rosser had sold their house in Hollywood and moved to Rancho Bernardo, not far from San Diego. The regular Tuesday night meditation was moved to Dennis and Gerry's new home, and Rose and I, Anne Marie Bennstrom, and several others attended regularly. With practice, I was now able to meditate for two hours fairly comfortably—especially in the presence of this group of seasoned meditators. I was also beginning to feel the results of practicing the presence of God—similarly known by psychologists as "mindfulness" or watching your thoughts and replacing negative ones with positive ones. Several times a year I attended weekend spiritual retreats, maintaining silence for the duration—which, at first, was a challenge. But throughout history, many great figures including

Gandhi have devoted one or more days to silence, thereby filling their nearly depleted spiritual reservoirs with God's power.

Dennis was slowly becoming a spokesman for saving the environment and believed in "walking his talk." He purchased land in Colorado not far from Telluride and began building his "Earthship"—a structure whose mass and internal support came from old tires and aluminum cans, which were then covered with a final layer of adobe. Designed by Michael Reynolds and off the power grid, the Earthship faces south in order to draw the maximum amount of sunshine into the solar panels. Rose and I spent quite a bit of time watching the construction, and at night had the beautiful experience of sleeping in a tepee under the star-filled Colorado skies. When the structure was complete, an indoor vegetable garden was planted in a south-facing lengthy planter, providing tomatoes, cucumbers, lettuce, and you name it year round. I used to love watching it snow outside while eating fresh veggies from the indoor garden.

We used to love to drive from L.A. to the site—a two-day drive mainly through southern Utah, with its magnificent scenery of giant rock formations, aspen groves, and mountain streams. The autumn season was my favorite time to make the trip, when the quaking aspens turned yellow and the oak trees turned red—all set against the backdrop of a deep blue cloudless sky. As Yogananda expressed it: "God is not remote from His creation; He is always with us. You don't see the breeze, but you know it is there. He who made the breeze and us, He is here."[30]

WAYNE'S WORLD
AND NEW HORIZONS

Good morning, Gary. It's Michael Ostin from Warner Bros., with some great news for you. Mike Myers and Dana Carvey want to use 'Dream Weaver' in their upcoming film, *Wayne's World*." I received Michael's phone call one morning early in 1992. "I love waking up to this kind of news," I replied. "Tell me more." Michael continued, "You probably know that Mike and Dana have been using your song on *Saturday Night Live* during their *Wayne's World* sketch, when Madonna was one of their guests—she being their 'Dream Weaver.'" I instantly thought, "Now that's a stretch from the original spiritual meaning of the song, but it's not offensive and they are both very funny so I'll give the OK." The negative force of maya can be very tricky when it comes to making difficult decisions like this, but intuitively I felt this was the right choice.

Michael went on to tell me that they wanted me to do a remix of the original song for the movie. Unfortunately, the original master multi-track tape for the album *The Dream Weaver* had been lost, mislabeled, or misplaced. We spent days looking through all the master vaults at Warner Bros. with no luck. Consequently, I had to re-create the entire

song from scratch, which was a challenge but also a lot of fun. At Michael's suggestion, David Gamson co-produced the new version of the song with me. When the film was released, the album went straight to number 1. Needless to say, I was elated, since "Dream Weaver" now reached a whole new generation of fans in the 1990s, giving my career a huge boost.

Slowly, an interesting chain of events unfolded. With the advent of rap and hip-hop during the 1990s and 2000s, various well-known artists like Jay Z, Kanye West, Tone-Lōc, 3rd Bass, Salt-N-Pepa, Mýa, and techno DJ Armand van Helden began to sample my music. My songs were also covered by Chaka Khan, Joe Cocker, Anastacia, Judas Priest, Joan Osborne, and Eminem, to name a few. "Dream Weaver" was also used in the Milos Forman Oscar nominee *The People vs. Larry Flynt*, as well as in *Toy Story 3*, *The Good Guys*, and *Glee*. "Love Is Alive" was in *One Night at McCool's* and *Coyote Ugly*. Things were turning around in a very good way for my career.

Yoga teaches that we are what we think, and I had begun to use affirmations daily for what I wanted to achieve and how I wanted to feel. Yogananda was very much into using positive thinking to create success, and now it was working for me in a tangible as well as spiritual way. He expressed it so clearly when he wrote, "Realize that all the power you use—to think, to speak, and to act—comes from God, and that He is with you now, guiding and inspiring you. As soon as you actually realize that, a flash of illumination will come and fear will leave you. Sometimes the power of God comes like an ocean and surges through your being in great boundless waves, sweeping away all obstacles."[31]

Along with this interest in my catalogue beginning in the early nineties comes an interesting story involving an A&R meeting my son Dorian at Warner Bros. He was trying to get a record deal and was meeting with several labels at the time. Dorian has a great voice, in a similar direction to Brian McKnight, but he baffled the labels because

they were unsure how they would market him on the radio—whether as pop or R&B. It's so crazy that really good music gets overlooked nowadays because it doesn't fit into a certain category that radio will play. The person leading the meeting that day told Dorian that he wanted him to hear something that the label was really excited about. It was a track by a new artist named Mýa called "Movin Out." Dorian listened politely, and when the track ended, he smiled and said, "Is that a Gary Wright bass line that they're using on the record? Because that's my dad's riff from his song 'Love Is Alive' that you're using as the backbone of the track." Surprised, the A&R executive quickly responded, "Wow, I didn't know that Mýa's producer used your dad's riff. I'll pass that through the proper channels to make sure the marketing and publicity people know about this."

The song became a big hit for Mýa, and had Dorian not been at that meeting, I might have never known my song had been used. During this period, music of many artists was sampled—myself included—without getting permission first from the artists, record labels, or music publishers. That changed quickly when litigation was threatened. Now it's standard practice for labels to go through the proper channels whenever songs are sampled so that artists can be fairly compensated for allowing their music to be used on new recordings.

It had been almost seven years since I had released the album *Who I Am* and I was feeling the urge to create again. I was still a big fan of world music and wanted to delve even deeper into that. I had all those boxes of tapes from my trip to Brazil in 1979, collecting dust in my studio. It was time to create an album around those fiery rhythms that were originally African based. The chanting and choral music that came out of Nigeria was very appealing to me and, coincidentally, I had recently met a Nigerian musician, Ayo Adeyemi through a musician friend of mine, Franz Pusch. Franz wound up coproducing the album with me, along with Marlon Klein and George Landress. After some

Gary and Dorian in South India, circa 1990.

thought, it became clear to me that I could use my Brazilian rhythm tracks along with African vocals—blending the cultures of Africa, Brazil, and even southern India.

The lyrics on the album, which would become *First Signs of Life* (released 1995), were sung in Nigerian. Ayo had helped me translate them into his language, with the exception of three tracks that I sang in English. The songs were all about God, and Ayo and I stacked up our vocal tracks in the studio to make it sound like a large group of singers. I played the bass and synth parts throughout the album, and one of the tracks—a world music pop song titled "Don't Try to Own Me"—featured Terry Bozzio (drums), Jimmy Haslip (bass guitar), and Steve Farris (guitar). The south Indian percussion on the track came from one of the songs on my *Who I Am* album, which we sampled. Acoustic

guitars on two tracks were played by Ricardo Silviera and Bernhard Locker. I shot a video for the track "Don't Try to Own Me" and George sang backing vocals with me in the choruses. A director friend of mine, Michael Schultz, kindly offered to direct the video and I was very pleased with the results. Ayo was very kind and helpful in the making of this record, not only in his singing, but in his translations and percussion playing on several tracks as well. Willy Bogner shot the photo that was used for the front cover.

Gary with Sônia and Willy Bogner at Gary's 70th birthday party.
(Photo by Rose Wright.)

When the album was released, I made a personal appearance on *The Tonight Show* with Jay Leno. I asked Steven Stills if he wanted to play guitar and sing backing vocals on the choruses, and he agreed. He graciously let me use his backing band as well, and Justin and Dorian sang backing vocals. Jay joked with my sons, remarking, "Gee, when I was a kid I had to wash my dad's car or mow the lawn to make extra money. You probably get your allowances singing with your dad and probably complain, 'Oh no, we have to sing with dad again on TV, what a drag.'"

Shortly after *First Signs of Life* was released, I met Oliver Leiber,

who at the time was Paula Abdul's producer. His dad was Jerry Leiber, from the famous writing and producing team Leiber and Stoller, who wrote and produced massive hits during the sixties. One day Oliver called me out of the blue to invite me to go see him play at a club in Beverly Hills. "We have a great band and people come up all the time and sit in or sing with us," he told me. "They would love it if you sang 'Dream Weaver' and 'Love Is Alive.'"

Quite frankly, the thought of getting onstage and performing live again made me nervous; it had been nearly eighteen years since I stopped doing concerts. Yet, another part of me said go ahead and have some fun. I did and really enjoyed it, and the crowd seemed to really like it as well. That's all it took to get me motivated to perform live again; I felt the time was now right and that I had grown and matured to a new level, where I would be able to give more to my audiences. I put a band together and started playing live again—really enjoying it.

The passage of time does interesting things to people's perception of things. Both "Dream Weaver" and "Love Is Alive" were still in hot rotation at the classic rock stations all over the country. Moreover, with the exposure I was getting from the films, TV shows, and covers by other artists, people were starting to refer to my songs as "classics." But the real reward for me came when I would finish a show and afterward, while signing autographs, was able to listen to the many stories fans related to me about how "Dream Weaver" played an important part in their lives—stories like "that was the song we played at our wedding" and "I was going through a very tough time in my life, and listening to your song inspired me not to end my life." I was moved—many times profoundly so—by these experiences I was hearing. Inwardly, I would thank God for the privilege of helping these souls in my own humble way, while trying not to let the ego get in the way. I was beginning to put into practice what my guru many times said about service to others: one should try every day to help someone whom others pass by, giving

words of encouragement or turning them to God. It was truly uplifting to be able to apply the wonderful philosophy I had learned over the years to my life's work. Somehow it made all the rough times I'd gone through in my own life OK.

In 1999, I released *Human Love*, more of a rock album with a distinct world music flavor, on my own new label, High Wave Music. I did a distribution deal with ADA, a company owned by Warner Bros. It was exciting to be able to make all the marketing and promotional decisions myself rather than be on a priority list of a major label—meaning their promotional budgets went to whoever they thought would sell the most, not because of the artistic value of the music. I used some of the same people who played on *Who I Am* and *First Signs of Life*, specifically Marlon Klein, Franz Pusch, and Bernhard Locker, who also helped in co-producing the album.

Jeff Lynne sang backing vocals with me on one of the tracks; L. Shankar sang and played Indian violin, and Lakshmi Shankar gave a stellar Indian vocal performance. Steve Farris and Bernhard Locker did most of the guitar work. Sergio González, who had played in my touring band, was on drums; and Jimmy Haslip and Tony Franklin were on bass guitar for two tracks. Several members from South African artist Johnny Clegg's band, Savuka, sang backing vocals on one of the tracks as well. I also did updated versions of two of my previously recorded songs, "The Wrong Time" from *Extraction*, and "Wildfire" from Spooky Tooth's *You Broke My Heart* album. Wyn Davis mixed the album at his studio, Total Access, in Redondo Beach. The album could not have turned out as it did without the help of Marlon Klein, a world music master who brought many of the elements together working from his home studio in Bielefeld, Germany, and in Los Angeles.

In the early 2000s, my son Justin asked me if he could record an album for my new label—not as a solo artist but as a rock band. I thought it was a good idea, as I wanted to release more albums on my

new record company, and he suggested the name "Intangible." I liked it, and he immediately began searching for musicians. After many auditions, he finally selected the band he wanted, and they started doing shows in and around L.A. Justin started writing songs and I immediately saw that his writing was very good—especially his unusual lyrical ideas. I encouraged him to keep writing until he had enough songs for an album. When it came time to start recording, I chose my friend Wyn Davis to engineer the project. Justin played most of the guitar parts and supervised the sessions as to what he wanted musically from the other musicians. When we started the vocals, he began to sing harmonies, many times stacking up his vocal tracks to create a rich texture. One time he came into the control room to listen to his backing vocal performance on one of the acoustic tracks he had recorded, and became overwhelmed emotionally at what he heard, amazed at what he had accomplished. I gave him a big hug, knowing what he was feeling, since I had felt that before in my earlier career. It was a special moment between us and I had a flashback to when Justin had sung on the track "I Am the Sky" on my "Light of Smiles" album in '75 when he was only four years old.

I had committed myself to take part in a celebrity golf tournament in New England with Dave Mason and some other artists. Having arrived from L.A. the day before, I was a bit jet-lagged and barely made it to the last bus transporting us to the golf course. I was the only passenger onboard, and just as the driver began pulling out, someone started shouting and pounding on the door, obviously wanting a ride to the course. Our new arrival introduced himself as Fred Curtis, and when I told him my name he recognized me and my work, and immediately launched into a passionate discussion about music. He invited me to

play golf that day in his group and I accepted. During the course of the day, I told him about my new record label and Justin's project. I told him I was looking for a partner to help me run the label and he seemed very interested in getting involved in the music business. He also had the financial wherewithal to help launch new projects, which would be vital to our success. He asked for a few days to consider my proposal, and after we parted I thought to myself, "Now what if I had taken an earlier bus? I never would have met Fred." I gave him some of Justin's music to listen to, and he called me a few days later and agreed to come onboard and play a part in the release of Intangible's new album. I was totally astonished at the chain of events that happened that day: our pure chance meeting, his love of music, and most important, his wanting to be involved in the project. Motivated by this windfall, I pulled out all the stops with connections I'd made over my years in the business and hired the best team to market and promote Intangible's new album. Fred and I spoke several times a day; he was a joy to work with. Together we arranged concerts for the band, as well as a comprehensive PR campaign. The first single got to number 30 in the Active Rock music charts, very decent success for a new artist given the climate of the record business at the time. Unfortunately, it stalled at radio and we lost the window of opportunity to have a hit single. Fred decided to move on, but his positive attitude was and still is an inspiration for me, and he is still a good friend to this day. Given the circumstances on how we first met, I can't help but think that our meeting was a karmic event.

I released two EP's and an instrumental ambient music album between 2005 and 2010, the first being *The Motion of Hidden Fire*, which contained a digital re-record of "Dream Weaver." Wyn Davis and I completely rerecorded the song digitally, adhering as closely as possible to the original version. The other four tracks on the EP were songs I'd written over the years that somehow were never recorded. Next I released *The Light of a Million Suns*, which featured a duet with my son

Dorian of a re-record of "Love Is Alive." It was an updated version of the song, and Dorian's vocal was truly great. We were recording his voice in my studio, and when we were finished, I closed my eyes and listened back to the entire track. When his vocal came in, tears welled up inside me at his performance. He sang vocal riffs and hit notes I only wish I could sing. It was a special moment in my life making that connection with my son.

In the early eighties, I recorded an album which at the time I called *Meditation Music*. This was before music was supercategorized into multiple genres as it is today. I used all my vintage analogue synths to create the textures I wanted, and each track flowed into the next, creating ambience. My goal was to have the music create visual pictures in the mind of the listener, and I even tried to name the tracks with images I felt coming from the music, titles like "Silent Choirs of Snowflakes" or "Stones, Stars and Sages." From time to time after I had finished recording the album, I would play it back at low volume on my home stereo system in various rooms of the house to create a peaceful atmosphere. But it wasn't until nearly twenty-five years later that I decided to release the album. To my astonishment, it started getting air play on the various cable radio channels throughout the country on their "atmosphere/ambient music" channels. I think God wanted me to wait till the time was right to release the album, which I named *Waiting to Catch the Light*.

Seventeen

THERE GOES THE SUN

n early 2000, I got the call from Linda Arias, George's sister-in-law, that George had become ill and may not be with us too much longer. I went to England with Rose to visit him. He was very positive and funny as always, with a great attitude toward his illness. He kept repeating to me, "We're not the body." As we walked around his garden, he showed us changes he'd made since the last time we were there, including a small Russian dacha surrounded by beautiful shrubs. He picked up a miniature acoustic guitar and started strumming a song he'd recently written—the same old George I'd known for years. I purposely avoided any reference to his condition, wanting to keep our conversation upbeat and positive, which was made easier by his joking and usual self. Deep down, however, I was very disturbed at the thought of losing my friend.

In November 2001, I saw George for the last time, in Switzerland. When Rose and I rang the bell to his home, the large door swung open and there he was, dressed like a Hare Krishna. I was wearing ankle-high cowboy boots, which he spotted immediately saying, "Aha, I see you're wearing Spanish boots." "Still the same old George," I thought to

myself, "not missing a beat." Although his life was coming to a close, he had a great attitude—even lucidly quoting passages from the Bengali saint Swami Vivekananda. My guru often said, "To be fit for Self-Realization, man must be fearless."[32] George was always fearless, and he manifested this quality right up to the end of his life. His wife Olivia's strength, patience, and loving attention to him was deeply inspiring as we all sat down for dinner together—our last supper. After the meal, he showed us recently taken videos of his garden back in England, pointing out the changes he had made since I last was there.

When I left, I was quite sure that this was the last time I would see him in this incarnation. I felt numb as Rose and I slowly drove away after our visit, not wanting to accept the inevitable. He was God's instrument in introducing me to my guru, and he helped the spiritual lives of many others all over the world through his lyrics and music. He passed away on November 29, 2001. I was recording in Florida when I got the news that he had left his body in great peace. As the media began reporting his passing, I saw a news feed from India of a large billboard with the words, "There goes the sun," a fitting tribute to this great soul. I felt a strong urge to do something special to mark the day of his passing, and decided to go into the studio and record a song we had written together in the early seventies called "To Discover Yourself." It had never been recorded before, and I played piano and sang the vocal, a simple and poignant way to honor the passing of my dear friend. I think it was probably the most beautiful song we ever wrote together.

While still living in my flat in Mayfair, I had started to write the song on my piano. I didn't have any lyrics yet. I asked George if he wanted to help me finish writing it and he agreed. He arrived at my flat one sunny spring afternoon and I played him what I had, humming the vocal melody over the chord changes I'd already written. He immediately pulled out his lyric pad and started writing words; I kept playing the melody over and over, until it was completed. He placed his lyric

pad on the piano and asked me to sing what he'd written. I was deeply touched by his words and thanked him again and again for the help. I never recorded the song but kept it in my heart till the right opportunity arose—his passing. I recently re-recorded "To Discover Yourself" in my studio, using my friends Robert and Dean DeLeo from Stone Temple Pilots on bass and guitar and Ringo on drums.

On many levels, George was a teacher and example for me. Here was someone who had everything—name, fame, wealth—and yet there was something still missing: that deep connection with God, which once awakened became more and more manifest in his life. I was blessed with the opportunity to see what that was like firsthand, so that I wouldn't have to go through the pain of unfulfillment by material attachments myself, only to realize that ultimately nothing can give you lasting, deep satisfaction unless your life is anchored in God awareness. According to Yogananda, you shouldn't let life cheat you; it's not necessary to go through every kind of experience in life to ultimately realize that only oneness with God will bring lasting satisfaction. Trying to find that joy in friends, career, family, luxury, or whatever is in reality the soul's deepest yearning to be once again united with God. Through the power of maya, or delusion, that endless seeking drives us to want this or that in the material world, and when we finally achieve success, whether it be financial or otherwise, our health and peace of mind are gone—a cruel lesson.

During the course of our friendship, I had harbored a desire to play onstage with him. Somehow that desire never came to fruition for one reason or another. But ironically, nearly thirty-eight years after I first met George, another Beatle, Ringo, invited me to play in his All-Starr Band. Having performed in four tours, including more than a hundred concerts all over the world, I would rank it with some of the best touring I've ever done—especially being onstage with Ringo while performing my songs "Dream Weaver" and "Love Is Alive." God satisfies

all our worthwhile desires, but not necessarily at the time we want them to happen. I had to wait thirty-eight years.

Ringo and I had first met when we played together on George's *All Things Must Pass* album in 1970. While I was still living in the U.K., we frequently met and recorded together on various projects like his first two singles—"It Don't Come Easy" and "Back Off Boogaloo," the *B.B. King in London* album, and George's subsequent solo albums. He immediately struck me with his warmth, friendliness, and great sense of humor. We lost contact after I moved back to the States and reconnected again in 2008 when he asked me to join the All-Starr Band on his upcoming U.S. tour. I was a member of the band in 2008 and 2010 in the United States, and in 2011 in Europe and South America. Throughout the time we worked together, I was always inspired by his performances, his drumming, and his attitude toward his fans. "Peace and love" was his mantra at the close of every show after we sang John Lennon's "Give Peace a Chance"; he was kind, thoughtful, and spiritual. I will always treasure that time in my life.

In June 2010, I released *Connected*, my first pop album since *Who I Am* over twenty years earlier. I composed most of the songs in my studio and wrote a lot of the lyrics during frequent trips to Colorado, driving through southern Utah in the fall and finding inspiration from the deep yellow quaking Aspen trees under a cloudless blue sky. Berklee College of Music graduate Rob Calhoun engineered the album and was a great sounding board for me during the recording and mixing processes. My friend Bobby Hart cowrote the track "Satisfied," which featured Ringo on drums, Jeff "Skunk" Baxter on rhythm guitar, and Joe Walsh on lead guitar. John Lang wrote the lyrics to "Gimme Some Time," and I cowrote "Life's Not a Battlefield" with Joe Beck, and "Can't Find No Mercy" with Oliver Leiber.

In the summer of 2006, Rose and I returned home from a trip to Sardinia, Italy, where we spend many of our summers with our German

Ringo, Rose, and Gary backstage in Vienna during a
tour with Ringo Starr's All Starr Band, 2011.

On tour with Ringo Starr's All Starr Band. *(© Rob Shanahan.)*

friends, George and Annette Simon-Moeller. As we arrived home after a long day, we found my son Justin and his wife, Stacy, waiting for us inside, which I felt was unusual. I was sensing that they were about to tell me something very important. "Dad, do you know anyone who was born on April 22?" he asked me. Confused and severely jet-lagged I answered, "I really don't, why?"

"You do now, because we're expecting our first child on or around that date, Grandpa and Grandma."

It took a while for his announcement to register with me, and I really had not thought too much about becoming a grandfather until Kirra Layne was actually born. Then my whole life was turned around. I had raised two boys, but girls have a totally different energy and I soon became hooked. As I sang to her and rocked her while she had her bottle, she would look up at me with her big blue eyes and I would smile back at her—a precious moment in time. I can only describe her as a gift of love from God. Fresh from the heavenly realms, small children sense the wonder and fascination of nature. It's beautiful to see creation through their eyes—especially their attraction to flowers. I wrote a song about her and called it "Kirra Layne," which was one of the tracks on my *Connected* album. She also has a beautiful voice, and when she first started to sing, she was in tune and had a perfect vibrato. Now she even makes up her own songs and lyrics as the mood strikes her, and she sometimes sings in a strange language from time to time—perhaps bringing her talent over from a recent incarnation as an opera diva. In my garden with me planting or weeding, she'll start singing in a sweet soprano voice while touching the flowers. It's like having Snow White there beside me.

Shortly before Kirra turned five, her younger sister, Aubrey, was born and will soon be turning two. Very different from Kirra and wonderful in her own way, she's just starting to learn how to sing, and loves it when I play the piano while she and Kirra dance around the living

room. If I stop playing, she gets mad and runs up to me shouting, "More, Papa, more." I also wrote a song for her, simply titled "Aubrey," which I sing to her when I rock her to sleep. I feel so blessed that God has given me this experience of having grandchildren, opening my heart to a newly discovered precious and tender love.

My life has been filled with so many special moments where I have felt that connection, that love, that joy of living in the presence of God. I thank Him every day for my wife, family, friends, musicians, writers, singers, and of course my guru and SRF. In this incarnation, I was given the role of a Dream Weaver, weaving my own personal dreams through my music and relationships with others, while ever watching the great Dream Weaver weave His. I try to always make the connection with Him while I weave my own dreams. Recently I introduced Kirra to Amanda Miguel and her husband, Diego Verdaguer, my two dear well-known artist friends from Argentina. We were at one of their shows in Los Angeles, backstage in their dressing room before their performance. Kirra, only six at the time, didn't know anything about their careers and innocently asked Amanda how she became famous. Amanda took her hand and said, "God gave me the gift of a voice and I thank Him every day for it." I think Kirra intuitively knew what she meant, and she put her little arms around Amanda's waist and gave her a hug as if to say, "I feel the same way about God, too." Kirra told me that she wants to be a singer when she grows up, and if I'm still alive, she wants to sing with me at my concerts. I told her, "I'll be alive, don't worry." Then she said, "Pinkie swear?" and I answered teary-eyed and deeply moved, "Pinkie swear."

EPILOGUE

My guru often said, "To spend your time just playing with life and not finding God is wasting the divinely bestowed power within you. . . . Remember, it is you who must travel to the kingdom of heaven; it will not come to you by special delivery. Each man has to hie his own way alone."[33] Through our own struggle, we achieve that final state of bliss where all our karma has been burned up and there is no need to reincarnate again unless God wants us to return to help others gain their liberation. It's all His show, which He takes very seriously, and I feel very touched and honored that in this lifetime He has given me so much. Yes, there was struggle and there will continue to be struggle, but I am ready for it because He is with me struggling and overcoming as I play my role as a Dream Weaver in His great play.

ACKNOWLEDGMENTS

I would like to give my special thanks to the following individuals for all their help in making this project possible: Michelle Anthony; David Vigliano; Sara Carder; Joanna Ng; Chris Agajanian; Ed Arrow; Anthony Mattero; Ringo; Robert DeLeo; Dean DeLeo; Rob Calhoun; Wyn Davis; Justin, Stacy, Kirra, and Aubrey Wright; Dorian and Lehua Wright; George and Annette Simon; Rob Shanahan; Randall Wixen; Anthony Sargueta; and Olga Vezeris.

Special thanks to Olivia Harrison for her support and help in editing my photo collection of George.

To Paramahansa Yogananda; Self Realization Fellowship; and Lauren Landress for all the help, inspiration, and encouragement during the creation of this memoir.

And of course to Rose, without whom this book could never have been written.

NOTES

1 Paramahansa Yogananda, *Man's Eternal Quest*, Self-Realization Fellowship, Los Angeles, CA.

2 Ibid.

3 Paramahansa Yogananda, *Sayings of Paramahansa Yogananda*, Self-Realization Fellowship, Los Angeles, CA.

4 Paramahansa Yogananda, *Inner Reflections*, Self-Realization Fellowship, Los Angeles, CA.

5 Paramahansa Yogananda, *Wine of the Mystic*, Self-Realization Fellowship, Los Angeles, CA.

6 Paramahansa Yogananda, *The Divine Romance*, Self-Realization Fellowship, Los Angeles, CA.

7 Paramahansa Yogananda, *Autobiography of a Yogi*, Self-Realization Fellowship, Los Angeles, CA.

8 Paramahansa Yogananda, *Songs of the Soul*, Self-Realization Fellowship, Los Angeles, CA.

9 Paramahansa Yogananda, *Second Coming of Christ*, Self-Realization Fellowship, Los Angeles, CA.

10 Paramahansa Yogananda, *Journey to Self-Realization*, Self-Realization Fellowship, Los Angeles, CA.

11 Yogananda, *Sayings of Paramahansa Yogananda*.

12 Ibid.

13 Yogananda, *The Divine Romance*.

14 Yogananda, *Songs of the Soul*.

15 Ibid.

16 Yogananda, *Man's Eternal Quest.*

17 Yogananda, *Autobiography of a Yogi.*

18 Yogananda, *Man's Eternal Quest.*

19 Ibid.

20 Yogananda, *Autobiography of a Yogi.*

21 Yogananda, *Journey to Self-Realization.*

22 Yogananda, *Where There Is Light.*

23 Ibid.

24 Yogananda, *Autobiography of a Yogi.*

25 Ibid.

26 Yogananda, *The Divine Romance.*

27 Yogananda, *Where There Is Light.*

28 Ibid.

29 Yogananda, *Autobiography of a Yogi.*

30 Yogananda, *The Divine Romance.*

31 Yogananda, *Inner Reflections.*

32 Paramahansa Yogananda, *God Talks with Arjuna*, Self-Realization Fellowship, Los Angeles, CA.

33 Yogananda, *Man's Eternal Quest.*